Vintage Cakes

Tremendously good cakes for sharing and giving

Jane Brocket

with photography by Polly Wreford

For Phoebe

First published in 2012 by Jacqui Small LLP
an imprint of Aurum Press Ltd
7 Greenland Street
London NW1 0ND

ISBN: 978 1 906417 73 4

A catalogue record for this book is available from the British Library.

2014 2013 2012
10 9 8 7 6 5 4 3 2 1

Printed in China

PUBLISHER Jacqui Small
MANAGING EDITOR Kerenza Swift
PROJECT EDITOR Abi Waters
ART DIRECTION & DESIGN Sarah Rock
PHOTOGRAPHER Polly Wreford
PRODUCTION Peter Colley

contents

a slice of baking history

When it comes to baking vintage cakes, it's very reassuring to know that there is a veritable wealth of traditions and reliable recipes to guide and inspire you. It's this homely, comforting heritage that is at the heart of this book. The cakes featured here are those that have been made by generations of perfectly ordinary home-bakers to recipes that have been perfected over time, so there is very little that can go wrong. There is nothing new-fangled or experimental about them, no weird-and-wonderful flavour combinations, and they don't require difficult-to-find, esoteric ingredients or costly equipment. They are simply classic cakes and treats that can be made by anyone with basic baking skills, cakes that taste of fresh butter and eggs, sweet fruit and gentle spices, cakes that create delicious aromas in the kitchen as well as a lovely warm glow of pride in the maker.

This book offers a collection of favourite and fondly remembered cakes and baked treats, and brings together recipes from many different baking cultures and histories. Some of these recipes are very old and some are more recent, but all have been chosen on the basis of their popularity and their ability to induce a sigh of nostalgia, to evoke happy memories of cake-eating, and to prompt a desire to bake.

Just as vintage cake recipes have stood the test of time, so the utensils and ingredients they require remain very much unchanged. A generously proportioned mixing bowl, a handful of well-worn wooden spoons, an accurate set of scales and a variety of baking tins are pretty much all you need to get going. Once you have started baking vintage cakes, you will soon find that you have enough stocks of flour, sugar, butter and eggs plus all the delightful finishing touches such as pretty paper cases, colourful hundreds and thousands, glacé cherries, pastel candles and sweetshop sweets to be able to make a classic cake at the drop of a hat.

The joy of vintage cakes does not stop with the baking and eating, as they look wonderful when presented, served or given as gifts in true matching vintage style. It is no wonder that this vintage look is so appealing; it's delightfully mix-and-match, eclectic and charming and, very importantly, it's easy and affordable. After a few decades of being unloved, hidden in attics or given away for jumble sales, vintage china, textiles and cutlery are now being sought out by thrifty bakers and home-makers who appreciate their beauty, charm and usefulness. Pretty plates, cheerful hand-embroidered tablecloths, tall, tiered cake stands and graceful silver-plated cake forks can all be pressed into service once more to make cake-time, no matter how ordinary or spectacular the occasion, look and feel very special.

Home-bakers have never needed much of an excuse to get out the mixing bowl, and have always liked to have a good repertoire of recipes to hand to cover all types of cake-eating occasions. So in this book you will find little cakes for after-school treats for weary children, big cakes for hungry family gatherings, fancy cakes for stylish afternoon teas, centrepiece celebration cakes, and plenty of classics for the cake tin so that you are never short of a good slice for elevenses or when friends drop in. Many have a fascinating history, some are simply much-loved classics and favourites, and a few are relatively modern but with 'vintage' stamped all over them. But all are a way of celebrating good company, and life itself.

A generous spread of vintage cakes looks as tempting as it ever did, and now that we have modern ovens and equipment plus widely available quality ingredients, it's easier than ever to bake these delicious treats.

essential ingredients

One of the great things about baking vintage cakes is that they don't require long lists of ingredients, nor do they need exotic or hard-to-find products. Previous generations of bakers had a much more limited range of products available to them, and had to make do with what they could find. So certain ingredients appear time and again, and today the majority are widely available in the major supermarkets and food shops.

Nevertheless, modern versions of vintage recipes taste a little different to those made in years gone by, because the quality of so many basic ingredients has improved tremendously. Butter is infinitely nicer than margarine; there is no margarine in this book even though many bakers swore by it in the 1960s and 1970s, because before that time all bakers used butter in their cakes. Some will argue that margarine gives a light, moist sponge, but nothing tastes as good as butter. In addition, we can now choose from a wonderful range of sugars, eggs are fresh and long-lasting, and flour comes without the threat of lumps and weevils. Add to the list dried fruits that don't need to be picked over, nuts that don't require peeling, genuine vanilla extract rather than ersatz vanilla essence, fruity jam, fresh spices and generous tubs of thick double cream, and you will see that the modern baker is in a very fortunate position.

THESE ARE THE ESSENTIAL INGREDIENTS:

EGGS Unless otherwise stated, all the eggs used in the recipes are large, free-range eggs. Eggs can be safely kept at room temperature all year round. If you are not keen on this idea, keep your eggs in a cool place, but not the fridge.

BUTTER All the butter in these recipes is basic, salted butter (not butter salted with salt crystals, though, as this isn't good for baking). Unsalted butter has become very popular in baking and pastry-making, but you would never see it specified in vintage cake recipes as it was not widely available. Taste-wise, it tends towards blandness, and lightly salted butter gives much better taste results.

If you bake regularly, it makes sense to keep a pack of butter out at room temperature so you don't have to bother softening some every time you fancy making a cake (it will be fine for a couple of days, except in really hot weather).

If you find yourself wanting to bake but have only cold butter to hand, there are a few ways of softening it. A few moments in a microwave is a quick and easy method. Alternatively, cut the cold butter into cubes, place in a bowl standing in hot water, and warm gently, creaming it with a wooden spoon as it softens. The easiest way, though, is to cut it into cubes and press it between your fingers and palms, using the natural warmth of your hands to soften it.

SUGAR You can make most cakes with caster sugar, but it's worth using the various sugars specified in the recipes as they have been chosen to make a significant difference to flavour and texture.

White caster sugar is the standard type, but golden caster sugar, which is now easy to find, gives excellent results in cakes.

Light soft brown sugar is the second most used sugar in this book, and it's a wonderful product. Sludgy and lightly caramel in flavour, it's excellent in light fruit cakes and richer, heavier sponges. It is interchangeable with light muscovado sugar, which is a little drier and finer.

Vintage cakes are made with simple, fresh ingredients and kitchen cupboard staples. It's worth using good-quality butter, sugar and flour, and free-range eggs as they make all the difference to the taste and texture of a cake.

Dark soft brown sugar is marvellous for rich fruit cakes and very dark sponges. It can be substituted with dark muscovado sugar, which tends to go hard very quickly.

Demerara sugar is mostly used as a crunchy topping these days, and rarely in cakes themselves. It is not essential, although it's good to have a packet in the cupboard and it keeps very well.

Icing sugar is always white in this book, and although it is very fine and dry these days, sifting ensures you don't get lumpy icing.

Other important sweet ingredients are:

- **Honey** – when honey is specified, any basic, clear, runny honey can be used.
- **Treacle and golden syrup** are both by-products of the sugar-refining process. Molasses is very similar to treacle, but there is no direct substitute for golden syrup (corn syrup is not the same). Fortunately, golden syrup is now widely available around the world.
- **Condensed milk** should be the 'full' type (and not 'light' as this can ruin a recipe).

FLOUR Despite the vast array of flours on most supermarket shelves nowadays, the baker of vintage cakes needs only to stock their storecupboard with three main varieties: plain, self-raising and strong bread flour. Due to improved quality and milling processes, modern flours do not need to be sifted unless the recipe indicates it is necessary.

RAISING AGENTS You will also need yeast (fast-action or dried), baking powder, bicarbonate of soda and cream of tartar, which are all cheap and easy to find. All lose their efficacy with time and, once opened, should be replaced every six to nine months.

CLOCKWISE FROM TOP LEFT: sultanas; light soft brown sugar; dyed glacé cherries; icing sugar; undyed glacé cherries; desiccated coconut; chopped mixed peel; and dark soft brown sugar.

DRIED AND GLACÉ FRUITS With their excellent keeping qualities, dried and glacé fruits have always been a boon to bakers. The most popular in vintage cake recipes are raisins, sultanas, currants, dried peel and glacé cherries. If you prefer, you can use bags of mixed dried fruit, although some recipes call for a specific fruit. You can also make substitutions and use any of the more modern dried fruits now available.

If you can find them, the pieces or strips of candied lemon and orange peel handmade in the traditional way are full of flavour with a dense, sticky texture, but they are expensive. Alternatively, you could make your own or use the little tubs of ready-chopped peel, which are fine but not top quality.

Although previous generations of bakers used the dyed, bright-red variety of glacé cherries, the modern deep-red, undyed cherries have a markedly better texture and flavour.

The dates used in the book are medjool dates, which have a plump, sticky texture and delicious, fudgy taste, and are worth using instead of the ready-chopped variety.

LEMONS Lemons are an indispensable ingredient in cakes and are best stored in the fridge where they will keep well for several weeks. Unwaxed lemons are preferable for zesting — or wash waxed lemons thoroughly before using. The same goes for oranges.

NUTS Nuts feature prominently in vintage cakes, and it's worth always having a bag of flaked and whole almonds in the cupboard as almonds are the most frequently used. You can grind the flaked or whole almonds yourself if a recipe calls for ground almonds, or buy them ready-ground. As nuts go off quite quickly, it's best to buy other types such as walnuts, hazelnuts and pecans as and when you need them.

DAIRY PRODUCTS When a recipe requires milk, you should use full or semi-skimmed milk, but not skimmed milk. In this book, cream is usually double, and all cream cheese is full fat.

FLAVOURINGS Vintage cakes seldom require unusual flavourings. However, when any flavouring is required, it is worth buying high-quality as poor imitations can spoil an otherwise good cake.

Cocoa should be good-quality cocoa powder and not drinking chocolate.

When a recipe calls for dark chocolate, you need decent chocolate with a minimum 70% cocoa solids.

When coffee is required, use powdered coffee or coffee granules.

Although it's fun to experiment with different spirits, in general brandy is the most useful.

Always look for genuine vanilla and almond extracts rather than flavour essences. They cost a lot more, but are very long-lasting and worth every penny.

Ground spices lose their flavour quickly once opened, so buy in small quantities, check freshness before using, and replace regularly. Commercial mixed spices are fine. An exception should be made for nutmeg, which is best bought whole and grated on a fine grater as required. It's also a good idea to buy other spices (cloves, cardamom, allspice) whole and grind them when needed.

DECORATIONS In the past, bakers and cake-eaters got excited about pastel candles, silver balls and hundreds and thousands, something that now seems quaint when we see our modern supermarket shelves full of colourful, whimsical cake decorations. Adding the finishing touches to your cakes is a matter of personal taste, but this can be a time to go wild, have fun and create fantastic flourishes.

FOOD COLOURING PASTE Vintage iced cakes were generally either white or pink, the latter thanks to cochineal, which was the only widely available food colouring. Now we have a brilliant selection of colours to choose from in the form of the concentrated food colouring pastes (available from specialist cake decorating suppliers). These are far better than the liquid colourings, as only a tiny amount is needed, and you can obtain really deep colours should you wish.

essential equipment

As with any enjoyable practical activity, there is a wealth of attractive, pleasing equipment a baker can amass and collect. But the reality is that you do not need a huge amount to get started. First and foremost you need an oven that functions, and if you are not sure about the settings, use an oven thermometer to check the heat levels as it is vital to bake cakes at the correct temperatures. Then you need a mixing bowl or two, a wooden spoon, a large metal spoon or flexible spatula, a sharp knife, a cake tin, and that is it. Everything else can be improvised, found elsewhere in the kitchen or bought as you go along.

However, if you are starting from scratch and need a checklist of general equipment, this is what I would recommend:

GENERAL EQUIPMENT

- A mixing bowl is essential, and the classic, pale-brown Mason Cash mixing bowls, which were designed with baking in mind, are the best. Buy the largest size you can find – you will be using it a lot.
- Small and medium-sized bowls: one or two of each, made from Pyrex, are invaluable for holding ingredients, making small mixes and melting chocolate.
- Flexible spatulas are possibly the most useful new utensil of the last few years. Made from silicone, they are heat-resistant, washable and marvellously flexible for scraping bowls, but also great for folding in, spooning out, levelling surfaces and spreading fillings.
- A wooden spoon is still cheap, cheerful and very useful for creaming, beating and stirring. It's also the very vintage way of doing things, and works as well as anything.

- If, however, your budget stretches a little further, you will never regret buying a handheld electric mixer that makes light work of mixing and whisking. If you are very keen on baking and ready to splash out, it may be worth investing in a free-standing mixer. The one thing that is not necessary for baking is a food processor.
- If you don't have an electric mixer of any sort, you will need a metal, handheld whisk for whisking egg whites and cream.
- A small coffee grinder is very useful for grinding nuts, breadcrumbs and spices. If you don't have one, simply buy ready-ground.
- A sieve is vital for sifting cake ingredients together and making icing sugar completely lump-free.
- Electronic scales are worth every penny they cost. They are accurate, ingredients can be weighed on them in any container (thus cutting down on washing-up) and they take up very little space.
- A sharp knife is useful for slicing, chopping, testing cakes for doneness and slicing cakes into layers.
- A pair of kitchen scissors is necessary for cutting out baking parchment for lining tins, chopping up candied peel and opening bags of ingredients (instead of pulling them apart and watching the contents fly everywhere).
- Another way to test for doneness is to use a metal skewer – very cheap and very useful.
- A fine grater is invaluable for grating nutmeg and zesting lemons. Microplane graters are the best – small, easy to clean and they stay sharp.
- A Pyrex jug for measuring liquids. Pyrex is difficult to break and lasts for years.
- You will need a small heavy-based saucepan for melting ingredients, and also a large heavy-based pan for melting, mixing and heating larger quantities.

The equipment required for baking vintage cakes has changed very little over the years, and is often just the same as our grandmothers used. It's easy to find and long-lasting, and you may soon find yourself deeply attached to favourite spatulas and sieves, jars and jugs.

- A free-standing timer in addition to the timer on the oven. It can be taken out of the kitchen so you can still be sure of knowing when to check a cake.
- You will need a good pair of oven gloves; tea towels may seem like a good idea, but they don't allow you to hold a hot tray for longer than a few moments. The huge, ultra-safe 'gauntlet' type of oven gloves offer excellent protection.
- And finally, an apron with a bib (one that goes over your head). Not because we should all act out some vintage domestic fantasy, but because an apron is fantastically practical, and the best way of keeping you and your clothes clean and protected. Choose one with a front pocket for carrying a timer.

USING WHAT YOU HAVE

It's very easy to get carried away with the beautiful, nonstick bakeware that is now widely available, and to feel that you must buy the right tin for every cake. In truth, you do not need many tins to make the cakes in this book. And if you don't have the one specified in a recipe, you can bake your cake in a slightly different size tin as long as you adjust your timings accordingly. So a 23cm cake can be made in a 20cm tin – but it will be deeper and need longer in the oven. Shapes are interchangeable, and any square/round/loaf/bundt cake can be made bundt/loaf/round/square. It is also possible to make a large cake as individual cakes and vice versa – just be sure to estimate new cooking times.

Wire cooling racks are one of the best investments a baker will make. Look for sturdy, strong, rectangular racks that are large enough to hold two cake tins and won't buckle with regular use. It's worth having at least two, as you'll need them when you are baking batches of cakes. Vintage racks are hard to find but can be beautiful – and useful.

As long as it is airtight, any tin can be used for storing cakes. Vintage tins are always attractive; if they are a little worse for wear on the inside, line them with baking parchment. A large deep tin is invaluable for special cakes, and it's now possible to buy cake boxes and containers that double as cake-carriers.

AND HERE IS A LIST OF SPECIALIST BAKING EQUIPMENT:

- Two solid, nonstick baking sheets.
- A 20cm nonstick deep round cake tin.
- Two 20cm nonstick round sandwich tins.
- A 23cm nonstick round springform or cake tin.
- A 20cm nonstick deep square cake tin.
- A 20cm nonstick shallow square tin (for brownies, gingerbread, various cakes).
- A 30 x 20cm Swiss roll tin.
- A couple of muffin trays for making muffins, cupcakes and fairy cakes.
- A shallow jam tart tin is useful for Maids of Honour (see page 111).
- A medium loaf tin about 20–22cm long, 10–12cm wide and 7cm high.
- A large loaf tin about 24cm long, 14cm wide and 7cm high.
- Two sturdy rectangular wire cooling racks that can hold a baking sheet or two cakes each.
- A roll of baking parchment for lining tins, rolling up Swiss rolls, catching drips of icing and wrapping up cakes. The usefulness of baking parchment cannot be overstated (it is much better than greaseproof paper).
- An assortment of cake and muffin paper cases – or just use plain white.
- A palette knife or a knife with a round end is the best thing for icing cakes, and for running round the edges of cakes in tins to loosen them to get them out.
- A rolling pin is very good for rolling out dough and breaking up biscuits, but a clean bottle will do just as well for the former and you can use your foot for the latter.

OPTIONAL EXTRAS:

Once you have established that you enjoy baking, there are plenty of lovely extra baking accessories and pieces of equipment you can spend your money on. These include:

- Bundt tins and beautifully shaped cake tins.
- A 24–25cm tube tin (also known as an Angel Food cake tin – see page 120).
- A madeleine tin. This could be classed as essential if you make a lot of Madeleines (see pages 156–57).
- Dariole moulds (but a muffin tin will work).
- A larger collection of round, square and loaf tins in a variety of sizes.
- A rolling pin.
- A tin of round cutters in various sizes. It's possible to use any round implement in the kitchen to cut out, but these do the job very well.
- A sugar thermometer is essential for Doughnuts (see page 69) but is not widely used elsewhere in the making of vintage cakes.
- A piping bag and set of icing nozzles are worth buying if you feel your talents and interests lie in the field of cake-decorating. Otherwise, all the cakes in this book can be covered and decorated without special equipment, and when a piping bag is needed, it can be improvised from a polythene bag.

HOW TO LINE CAKE TINS

Modern nonstick cake tins and baking equipment really are nonstick, so in theory it's not absolutely necessary to line them. However, in practice, it pays to line a tin, especially for cakes that are very damp or require a long baking time. It only takes a few moments to line a tin and it means that your cakes will come out of their tins quickly and easily, and without any sponge sticking to the base. Even if you only line the base, it will make a difference.

To line a tin, use baking parchment (buy it by the roll). The easiest way is to stand the cake tin on the paper, draw round it and cut it out just inside the lines so that it will be able to fit snugly in the tin. Then cut out strips to line the sides. To line a loaf tin, brownie tray or Swiss roll tin, place the tin on the paper and draw round the base. Cut out the rectangle or square allowing enough paper to cover the sides. Then cut out a square at each outside corner so that you can cover the base and fold the side sections up the sides of the loaf tin.

essential techniques

What rules there are in baking are very simple and sensible. Baking works when recipes are followed; it's not like cooking where it's possible to improvise endlessly. Of course, you can substitute flavours, change sugars, alter fruit mixes, but ultimately you should stick closely to the quantities of ingredients specified and bake at the given temperature. While this adherence to a set of instructions may restrict creativity, it does make baking very easy. And once you have mastered a few simple techniques, you will be able to make everything in this book, no matter how inexperienced a baker you are.

OVEN TEMPERATURE All the temperatures given in the recipes are for conventional ovens. However, temperatures can vary from oven to oven, and if you are not sure of the exact temperature your oven is reaching on any given setting, it is worth buying an oven thermometer to check and to monitor, so that you can make suitable adjustments. In vintage recipes there were usually directions for which shelf to use, but as modern ovens are much more consistent, the middle is generally the best place to bake all cakes.

USING YEAST When you are working with yeast for recipes such as Doughnuts (see page 69) and Chelsea Buns (see page 105), there is a basic method to follow as you will need to make a yeast starter to begin with. Put the yeast and sugar in a medium bowl. Gently heat the milk or water to blood temperature (no hotter) and pour over the yeast. Mix, then add 100g of the flour and mix again. Leave for 20 minutes until gently frothy. If it does not froth, the yeast is not working and you should start again with a fresh batch. Now carry on with the recipe as instructed.

CREAMING When a recipe says to 'cream butter and sugar together' this means mixing them well to make a smooth, creamy mixture, which turns paler in the process. A wooden spoon does the job well, but it's much easier and faster with an electric mixer.

BEATING The aim of beating or creaming is to introduce as much air as possible into a mix. So it should be done vigorously, whether by hand or with an electric mixer. It helps enormously if you stop a couple of times in the process to scrape down the sides of the bowl (a flexible silicone spatula is the best way to do this) to ensure all the ingredients are incorporated evenly.

RUBBING IN 'Rubbing in' is the process of mixing butter and flour (and sometimes sugar) until it looks like sand or breadcrumbs, usually to make pastry or crumble toppings. Cut the butter into cubes, pick up a couple of cubes at a time with a small quantity of flour and rub quickly and gently between your fingers, letting the ingredients fall back into the bowl. Repeat until all the fat has been rubbed into the dry ingredients. For best results, use cold butter, but if you have no cold butter available, it's very easy to rub in soft butter as long as you work quickly and lightly.

SCRAPING DOWN While you are mixing, beating, whisking and folding, scrape down the sides of the bowl with a flexible spatula so that all the ingredients are evenly combined. If you are using an electric mixer, switch off the power a couple of times during mixing in order to scrape down. Make sure you run the spatula over the bottom of the bowl as there can sometimes be a layer of unmixed ingredients there.

SIFTING Sifting has two purposes: to remove lumps and to increase the amount of air in a mix. Nowadays, it is not always necessary to sift flour as it is much finer and better quality. However, sometimes it pays to sift, especially if you are making a very airy, fluffy cake such as Swiss Roll (see page 140), French Macaroons (see page 152) or Chiffon Cake (see page 120). It is always worth sifting icing sugar; no matter how fine it is, it tends to clump when liquids are added.

WHISKING Whisking is another way of incorporating air into a mix or ingredients, such as egg whites, egg yolks or cream. A simple metal whisk does the job well, although it takes a lot of wrist action and energy. For fast and even results, a handheld electric or free-standing mixer is invaluable.

Don't worry too much about 'peaks' but concentrate instead on the texture of the whisked mix and whether it holds a soft, billowing shape (i.e a 'soft peak'). Most of the time, this is all you need to achieve with egg-white mixes as over-whisking can make the mix dry and gritty. Similarly with cream, it is very easy to over-whisk and end up with stiff cream that is hard to spread, so it is better to stop as soon as you find the cream is holding its shape nicely without being too runny or too firm.

FOLDING IN Once you have carefully beaten and maybe sifted, you want to retain all the air in the mix while adding the rest of the ingredients. 'Folding in' is the method of mixing very gently to maintain the air content. With a large metal spoon or flexible spatula, simply scoop up spoonfuls of mix and fold them over gently, repeating the action until all the ingredients are combined. Some people use a figure–of–eight motion, others simply turn the bowl as they work. Use the same utensil to spoon the mix carefully into the tin then level the surface lightly with the back.

ADDING COLOUR Use a cocktail stick or toothpick to add small amounts of food colouring paste to a mix. Discard the toothpick or cocktail stick and use a new one for each addition.

TESTING FOR DONENESS Although some bakers can tell a cake is done just by touching the surface, it's better to judge by a combination of factors. Generally speaking, a cake that is done will be golden brown on top, feel firm and springy to the touch, and the edge will be pulling away from the tin. However, the most reliable way to test it is with a metal skewer or small, sharp knife. Open the oven, pull the cake towards you on the shelf (don't take it out of the oven completely or it may sink) and insert the skewer or knife into the centre. If it comes out clean, with no trace of uncooked mixture on it, the cake is done. If the centre is not yet cooked, return the cake to the oven and check at intervals until done (setting a timer if necessary to remind you).

It's not so long ago that there were such things as 'baking days' when ranges and ovens were fired up and the cake-maker of the house would spend a day baking in order to fill battered, oft-opened tins with big, spicy, fruit-filled cakes that would keep all week. We may not have the time or inclination to go back to full-on baking days, but there is a great deal to be said for having a cake in a tin, ready to slice, ready to share. There is also something terribly comforting and unfrantic about baking cakes to keep; our time is being invested in one of the nicest ways possible, and is repaid with dividends when we have the pleasure of cutting and knowing there is more for later. These keeping cakes, some of which improve with time, are often hearty cakes made to old, time-honoured recipes using classic ingredients that defy any thoughts of updating and modernisation. Although some are light, zesty, all-year-round favourites, many have associations with historical events and traditional, seasonal baking, and are truly a taste of vintage cake.

cake-tin cakes

Vintage recipes for marmalade cake have been in circulation for a long time. However, they tend to be rather plain and dry, so this is a softer, tastier, modern version. It makes a subtly orangey cake, not at all bitter, with a good texture and the occasional bite of candied peel, while the icing offers a contrasting hint of citrus to balance the sweetness. The style of marmalade is a matter of personal taste, so use whatever type you prefer, and if you can find it, traditionally made candied peel adds an extra touch of vintage flavour.

marmalade cake

FOR THE CAKE

175g soft butter, plus extra
    for greasing
175g light soft brown sugar
3 eggs
grated zest of 1 orange (unwaxed or
    well washed)
juice of ½ an orange
25g candied orange peel, chopped
    (optional)
3 rounded dessertspoons or 2 rounded
    tablespoons orange marmalade
200g self-raising flour

FOR THE ICING

150g icing sugar
juice of 1 orange

YOU WILL NEED

a 20cm round deep cake tin, greased
with butter and base lined with
baking parchment

makes 1 large cake
(serves 8–10)

1/ Preheat the oven to 180°C (gas mark 4).

2/ Put the butter and sugar in a large mixing bowl. With a wooden spoon or an electric whisk, cream them together until they are pale and fluffy. Add the eggs one by one, beating well after each addition.

3/ Add the grated orange zest and juice, candied orange peel (if using) and the marmalade and mix in gently with a large metal spoon. Sift the flour into the mix and fold in gently.

4/ Spoon the mix into the prepared tin, levelling the surface with the back of the spoon. Bake in the preheated oven for 40–50 minutes, but check after 30–35 minutes to make sure the top is not browning too quickly. If it is, cover the cake loosely with a double thickness of aluminium foil to prevent it burning. The cake is done when a metal skewer or sharp knife inserted into the centre of the cake comes out clean.

5/ Transfer the tin to a wire rack and leave the cake to cool for 5–10 minutes before turning out. Do not begin to ice the cake until it is completely cool.

6/ To make the icing, sift the icing sugar into a bowl and add half the orange juice. Mix thoroughly with a knife, gradually adding as much juice as necessary to give a spreadable, smooth but slightly runny consistency. Using a blunt-ended knife or palette knife, spread the icing over the surface of the cooled cake, allowing the icing to drip down the sides.

STORAGE: Marmalade cake is delicious on the day it is made, and will keep for a couple of days if wrapped in foil and stored in an airtight tin in a cool place.

The Scottish have a knack for creating very tasty exportable goods such as shortbread, marmalade and the classic Dundee cake. Lighter and crumblier than most rich fruit cakes, it's traditionally topped with a pattern of blanched almonds (although these are optional when making at home). It's an ideal cake-tin cake, one that will bring good cheer in the dark, cold days of winter when it can be brought out in the afternoon and enjoyed with a steaming-hot cup of tea.

dundee cake

FOR THE CAKE

170g plain flour
120g self-raising flour
½ teaspoon mixed spice
¼ teaspoon nutmeg, grated
60g ground almonds
150g glacé cherries
350g sultanas
250g raisins
grated zest of 1 lemon
250g soft butter, plus extra
    for greasing
250g light soft brown sugar
4 eggs
whole blanched almonds (optional),
    to decorate

YOU WILL NEED

a 20cm round cake tin, greased with butter and lined with baking parchment. Wrap a double or triple layer of newspaper or brown paper round the outside of the cake tin and tie tightly with string to prevent the cake burning while cooking. Use long strips of paper that are 1–2cm taller than the tin.

makes 1 large cake
(serves 12–14)

1/ Preheat the oven to 140°C (gas mark 1).

2/ First, prepare the dry ingredients. Sift the flours and spices into a bowl and stir in the ground almonds.

3/ Next, prepare the fruits. Rinse the glacé cherries in warm water, pat or shake them dry, slice in half and put in a second bowl with the sultanas, raisins and grated lemon zest.

4/ Put the butter and sugar in a large mixing bowl. With a wooden spoon or an electric whisk, cream them together until they are pale and fluffy. Add the eggs one by one, beating well after each addition.

5/ Tip in the flour mix and fruit and fold in gently with a large metal spoon, making sure all the ingredients are incorporated.

6/ Spoon the mixture into the prepared tin. Wet one hand with cold water and use the back of your hand to level the surface by pressing gently. Arrange the whole almonds on top (if using).

7/ Bake in the preheated oven for about 2¼–2½ hours or until a metal skewer or sharp knife inserted into the centre of the cake comes out clean. Leave the cake in its tin on a wire rack to cool before turning it out and wrapping it in foil.

STORAGE: Dundee cake keeps well for 7–10 days if wrapped in foil and stored in an airtight container.

Dates are a winter delight and a staple ingredient of that season's rich, dark fruit cakes. But they are at their best when they are allowed to shine on their own, and a cake dedicated to dates is a marvellous showcase for the fruit's sweet stickiness and thick, grainy texture. Cake-bakers have been making the most of these qualities for years, but now that the large, soft, sugary medjool dates are sold in supermarkets, we no longer have to rely on the small, papery dates that came in a wooden box with a little fork and were such a treat at Christmas.

sticky date cake

FOR THE CAKE

275g medjool dates, halved and
 chopped into sixths or eighths
175g raisins
225g sultanas
250g butter, plus extra for greasing
275ml water
1 x 397g tin condensed milk
300g plain flour
1 level teaspoon bicarbonate of soda
1 tablespoon orange marmalade

YOU WILL NEED

a 20cm round cake tin, greased with
butter and lined with baking parchment

*makes 1 large
cake (serves 10)*

1/ Put the chopped dates, raisins, sultanas, butter, water and condensed milk into a large, heavy-based saucepan. Heat gently until the butter has melted, stirring from time to time. (Do not overstir as this breaks up the dates.) Bring the mixture to the boil and then continue to boil over a medium, but not fierce, heat for 3 minutes, stirring from time to time to stop the mix sticking. After 3 minutes, it will turn a deeper colour and smell of caramel. Set aside in a cool place and leave until lukewarm or cool.

2/ When you are ready to bake, preheat the oven to 160°C (gas mark 3).

3/ Sift the flour and bicarbonate of soda into the saucepan of cooled fruit mixture and add the marmalade.

4/ With a large spoon or flexible spatula, mix together all of the ingredients until they are well combined. Spoon the mixture into the tin and level the surface with the back of the spoon or spatula.

5/ Bake for 2–2½ hours, but check that the cake is not browning too quickly after an hour. If it is, place a double thickness of aluminium foil over the top of the tin. The cake is done when a metal skewer or sharp knife inserted into the centre comes out clean.

6/ Transfer to a wire rack and leave to cool before turning out of the tin. Wrap well in foil or greaseproof paper and keep in an airtight tin in a cool place.

STORAGE: Sticky date cake keeps well for 7 days, wrapped as instructed in step 6.

cook's tip

After boiling the fruits, be sure to allow sufficient time for the mix to cool before proceeding to the next stage.

For many cake-lovers growing up in the North of England, dark, damp, spicy parkin will be forever associated with Bonfire Night on November 5th, and the smells and excitements of smoke and fireworks. It's a marvellously vintage treat with a long history, made with old-fashioned ingredients such as treacle, oatmeal and ginger. It tastes as good as it ever did, and to enjoy it at its best it should be made four to five days before you plan to eat it; that way it matures and improves. In the past, parkin was packed in special cases, but these days a cake tin will do: when you lift the lid you will be transported to a different era.

parkin

FOR THE CAKE

120g golden syrup

120g treacle

120g butter, plus extra for greasing

120g dark soft brown sugar or dark muscovado sugar

220g fine oatmeal (not medium, which is too coarse)

120g self-raising flour

2 teaspoons ground ginger

a pinch of salt

50ml milk

1 egg, lightly beaten

YOU WILL NEED

a 20cm square cake tin, lightly greased with butter and lined with baking parchment

makes 16 squares

1/ Preheat the oven to 160°C (gas mark 3).

2/ Put the syrup, treacle, butter and sugar in a large saucepan. Heat gently until the butter has melted, stirring frequently. When the sugar has dissolved and you have a smooth liquid, remove the pan from the heat and leave to cool for a few minutes.

3/ Put the oatmeal, flour, ground ginger and salt in a small bowl. Stir well to mix and then add to the saucepan. Add the milk and egg and mix well until you have a smooth batter.

4/ Pour into the prepared tin and bake in the preheated oven for 45–50 minutes until the top is firm to the touch and a metal skewer or sharp knife inserted into the centre of the cake comes out clean. Transfer to a wire rack and leave to cool before turning out of the tin.

5/ When cold, wrap the cake in greaseproof paper or aluminium foil and store in an airtight tin in a cool place.

STORAGE: Parkin is good on the day of making, but definitely improves with age and is often eaten 3–5 days after making.

gingerbread

The whole point of this type of gingerbread is that it should be dark, sticky, treacly and very gingery. Thanks to the availability and popularity of ginger over the centuries, it's one of the most vintage of all vintage cakes, with an illustrious history stretching back to the medieval 'gingerbread fairs' that were held in many European countries. The jellied lemon slices, the ones that seemed so posh in the 1970s, bring it into a different era, but in fact gingerbread never truly goes out of date.

gingerbread

FOR THE CAKE
150g butter, plus extra for greasing
150g dark soft brown sugar
100g golden syrup
200g treacle
300g plain flour
2½–3 teaspoons (slightly heaped) ground ginger
200ml milk, plus 1 tablespoon
2 eggs, lightly beaten
1 teaspoon bicarbonate of soda

FOR THE ICING
300–350g icing sugar
juice of 1–2 lemons (use oranges if you find lemon juice too tart)

TO DECORATE
16 jelly/candied lemon slices (optional)
OR orange slices (if using orange juice)
OR a few pieces of candied ginger or stem ginger

YOU WILL NEED
a 24 x 24cm square baking tin, greased with butter and lined with greaseproof paper or baking parchment

makes 16 squares

1/ Preheat the oven to 160°C (gas mark 3).

2/ In a large, heavy-based saucepan melt the butter, sugar, golden syrup and treacle, stirring regularly. Take off the heat and leave to cool for a few minutes.

3/ Sift the flour and ground ginger into a large mixing bowl. Measure out the 200ml milk in a measuring jug. Add the eggs to the milk and whisk to mix.

4/ When the butter mixture has cooled, mix the bicarbonate of soda with the remaining 1 tablespoon milk in a small bowl or tea cup (the mixture will start to fizz straightaway).

5/ Add the milk and egg mixture, the melted butter mixture and the bicarbonate of soda mixture to the dry ingredients in the large bowl. Mix together until it forms a well-mixed, quite runny batter with no lumps or as few flour lumps as possible.

6/ Pour the mixture into the prepared cake tin and bake in the preheated oven for 40 minutes until nicely domed and slightly pocked on top, and a metal skewer or sharp knife comes out sticky but without any uncooked mixture on it. Do not be tempted to overcook, as this gingerbread should be moist and slightly sticky. Leave on a wire rack to cool completely before icing (see tip below).

7/ Make the icing. Sift the icing sugar into a bowl and start adding the lemon juice and mixing with a knife. Continue adding and mixing until you have a glistening thick white icing that will spread but not drip.

8/ Cover the cake with the icing and place the lemon slices in a 4 x 4 row arrangement, so that the cake can be cut into 16 squares, each with a lemon slice on top.

STORAGE: Gingerbread keeps very well for up to a week. Store in an airtight tin in a cool place.

cook's tip
You can ice the cake in the tin before taking it out so that the icing doesn't run down the sides, but it is possible to remove the cake when cool and ice it on a plate or board.

Seed cake has been much maligned and mocked by a cake-eating public grown used to richer, fancier, fuller cakes. But we should not dismiss its subtle charms. As Mrs Beeton and many a recipe-writer before and after her knew, when seed cake is made well with fresh butter and eggs, it is a very grown-up, pleasing cake that works beautifully with a china cup of tea made with tea leaves (Darjeeling is particularly well suited to plain cakes) or with a small glass of chilled Madeira. The trick is to be sparing with the caraway seeds, so that their flavour is understated.

rich seed cake

FOR THE CAKE
180g soft butter, plus extra
    for greasing
180g caster sugar
4 eggs, separated
250g self-raising flour
2 teaspoons caraway seeds
2–3 tablespoons brandy or milk

YOU WILL NEED
a loaf tin, about 24 x 13 x 7cm, greased with butter and lined with baking parchment

*makes 1 large loaf
(serves 8–10)*

1/ Preheat the oven to 160°C (gas mark 3).
2/ Put the butter and sugar in a large mixing bowl. With a wooden spoon or an electric whisk, cream them together until they are pale and fluffy. Add the egg yolks and beat well to combine.
3/ Whisk the egg whites in a separate, clean bowl until soft peaks form. Add to the large bowl and fold in gently with a large metal spoon. Sift in the flour and add the seeds and brandy or milk, and continue to fold in gently until all the ingredients are evenly combined.
4/ Spoon the mixture into the prepared loaf tin and smooth the surface with the back of the spoon. Bake in the preheated oven for 45–55 minutes until well risen and golden brown, and a metal skewer or sharp knife inserted into the centre of the cake comes out clean. Transfer to a wire rack and leave to cool for 15 minutes before turning out of the tin. Serve fresh with tea or Madeira.
STORAGE: Seed cakes keep well for a couple of days if wrapped in foil and stored in an airtight tin.

It may sound simple and ordinary now, but it's not so long ago that a sponge flavoured with fresh oranges and filled with rich, buttery buttercream was regarded as a great treat, something to be baked for a birthday or for a special afternoon tea. It mixes sweetness with a touch of sophistication, and is particularly good when oranges are in season and plentiful and you are looking for an alternative to treacle, ginger and dried fruit. It can be left plain and simple, or it can be dressed up with sweets and candles. Orange sandwich cake is an often overlooked vintage cake, probably because it does not have a specific or historical name, but home-bakers always knew how to make it and it's a recipe that deserves its place in any baking repertoire.

orange sandwich cake

FOR THE CAKE

270g soft butter, plus extra
for greasing
270g caster sugar
4 large eggs, separated
finely grated zest and juice
of 1 orange (unwaxed or
well washed)
265g self-raising flour

FOR THE FILLING

200g icing sugar
60g soft butter
1–2 tablespoons fresh orange juice

FOR THE ICING

200g icing sugar
2–3 tablespoons fresh orange juice

YOU WILL NEED

two 20cm round cake tins, greased
with butter and lined with baking
parchment

*makes 1 medium–large cake
(serves 10)*

1/ Preheat the oven to 180°C (gas mark 4).

2/ Put the butter and sugar in a large mixing bowl. With a wooden spoon or an electric whisk, cream them together until they are pale and fluffy. In a separate, clean bowl, whisk the egg whites until soft peaks form.

3/ Add the egg yolks to the butter and sugar mixture one by one along with a little orange juice each time, beating well after each addition.

4/ Sift in the flour. Add the orange zest and the whisked egg whites. With a large metal spoon, gently fold in until all the ingredients are evenly and well combined, taking care not to knock air out of the cake mix.

5/ Divide the mixture equally between the 2 prepared tins. Level the surfaces with the back of the spoon. Bake in the preheated oven for 25 minutes until well risen and golden brown, and a metal skewer or sharp knife inserted into the centre of the cakes comes out clean.

6/ Transfer to a wire rack and leave to cool for 10 minutes before turning the cakes out of the tins. Leave until completely cool before filling and icing.

7/ To make the buttercream filling, sift the icing sugar into a medium-sized bowl and add the butter and 1 tablespoon orange juice. Mix well with a wooden spoon or flexible spatula until you have a smooth, spreadable consistency. Add more orange juice and/or icing sugar to achieve the consistency and taste you prefer.

8/ To make the icing, sift the icing sugar into a medium-sized bowl. Add 1 tablespoon of orange juice and start mixing well with a wooden spoon or flexible spatula. Gradually add more orange juice until you have a smooth, glossy and slightly runny consistency (not too runny, or it will just run off the cake).

9/ To finish the cake, put 1 layer of sponge upside down (so you get a level surface) on a cake plate or stand. With a palette knife (or ordinary knife), spread the buttercream over the surface. Place the second layer of sponge the right way up on top. With a palette knife and working from the centre, gently cover the surface of the cake with the icing, allowing it to drip down the sides of its own accord.

STORAGE: As with all light sponges, an orange sandwich cake is best eaten within 24 hours of making (it can be made a day in advance of a celebration) but will keep for another day if wrapped in foil and stored in a tin in a cool place.

Cherry cake is the epitome of cheerful, straightforward, unpretentious home-baking, and although vintage recipes suggest various ways of preventing the cherries from sinking, it just wouldn't be the same if they were all distributed perfectly. It is a simple, rich, buttery sponge, so to make it special it should be made with generosity; as generations of cake-eaters will know, there's nothing worse than counting the cherries in a cherry cake and finding them sadly lacking. This recipe makes a good-size cake with plenty of glacé cherries (a staple of vintage larders), which is ideal as an after-school treat or for sharing round a kitchen table with a big pot of tea. You can use vintage-style bright-red cherries to get the look, but modern, undyed cherries have a far better taste and texture, and turn an old favourite into a new classic.

cherry cake

FOR THE CAKE
200g self-raising flour
½ teaspoon baking powder
75g ground almonds
finely grated zest of 1 lemon
    (unwaxed or well washed)
275–300g glacé cherries (undyed if
    possible), plus 8–10 whole cherries
    to decorate (optional)
225g soft butter, plus extra
    for greasing
225g caster sugar
3 large eggs
a few drops of almond extract
    (optional)
1–2 tablespoons milk

FOR THE ICING (OPTIONAL)
200–250g icing sugar
juice of 1–2 lemons OR water to mix

YOU WILL NEED
a medium nonstick loaf tin, about
23 x 13 x 7cm, greased with butter

*makes 1 large cake
(serves 6–8)*

1/ Preheat the oven to 180°C (gas mark 4).
2/ Sift the flour and baking powder into a bowl and stir in the ground almonds and the lemon zest.
3/ Rinse the cherries in lukewarm water to remove any excess syrup. Pat dry with kitchen paper or a clean tea towel and slice each one in half. Add to the dry ingredients and toss gently to distribute, and to coat the cherries with flour.
4/ Put the butter and sugar in a large mixing bowl. With a wooden spoon or an electric whisk, cream them together until they are pale and fluffy.
5/ Add the eggs one by one, and a few drops of almond extract (if using), beating well after each addition.
6/ Add the dry ingredients together with the milk, and fold into the mixture with a large metal spoon or flexible spatula, making sure the cherries are well dispersed.
7/ Spoon the mixture into the prepared tin and bake in the preheated oven for 55–60 minutes. Check after 40 minutes and if the top is browning quickly, place a double thickness of aluminium foil on top of the cake. The cake is done when a metal skewer or sharp knife inserted into the centre of the cake comes out clean.
8/ Place on a wire rack and leave to cool before turning out of the tin.
9/ When completely cool, make your chosen icing (if using). Sift 200g of the icing sugar into a bowl. Gradually add lemon juice or water to taste and mix well with a knife until you have a thick, smooth consistency of icing that doesn't drip down the sides (unless that is the look you'd like). Add more icing sugar if necessary to thicken or to increase the quantity.
10/ Spread the icing thickly on top of the cake. Leave it to settle for a few minutes then decorate with whole glacé cherries if desired. Serve in thick slices.
STORAGE: Cherry cake is delicious on the day it is made, but keeps well for 2 days if stored in an airtight tin in a cool place.

Nutmeg is a supremely vintage spice, with its very own history associated with small, sweet-smelling spice-boxes, tiny graters and pale-green tins with 'nutmeg' printed on them. Most commonly, it's an ingredient in a mixed-spice blend, but it is worth using on its own for its gentle, evocative qualities. Nutmeg cake is a traditional Armenian favourite that is now popular in Australia. It's a little different to most cakes as it has a pastry-style base with a firm sponge on top. It's worth baking just to fill your house with a warm, nutmeg fragrance, but it's also tastes delicious and keeps well.

nutmeg cake

FOR THE CAKE

220g self-raising flour
330g light soft brown sugar or light
    muscovado sugar
125g cold butter, cubed, plus extra
    for greasing
2 teaspoons grated nutmeg
250ml milk
1 egg, lightly beaten
1 teaspoon bicarbonate of soda

YOU WILL NEED

a 23cm round or springform cake tin, greased with butter and base lined with baking parchment

*makes 1 large cake
(serves 10–12)*

1/ Preheat the oven to 180°C (gas mark 4).

2/ Put the flour and sugar in a large mixing bowl and stir to mix. Add the butter. With your fingertips, rub the butter into the flour and sugar until the mixture resembles fine sandy breadcrumbs. Tip one-third of the dry mix into the cake tin and press down lightly to level (do not press too firmly). Add the nutmeg to the remaining dry mix in the bowl and combine well.

3/ Measure out the milk in a jug. Add the egg and the bicarbonate of soda and mix lightly. Pour the liquid into the mixing bowl with the rest of the dry ingredients and stir lightly to mix. Pour the batter over the base of the cake in the tin.

4/ Bake in the preheated oven for 40 minutes until the cake is firm and springy to the touch, and a metal skewer or sharp knife inserted into the centre comes out clean. Transfer to a wire rack and leave to cool before turning out of the tin.

STORAGE: Nutmeg cake is delicious while still warm and on the day of making, but keeps well for 2 days if stored in an airtight tin in a cool place. It also freezes successfully.

cook's tip

Buy whole nutmegs so you can grate them yourself on a fine grater. Avoid ready-ground nutmeg as it loses its freshness very quickly.

No matter where in the world you are, every apple-growing country and region has its own local version of fresh apple cake enshrined in a recipe that has been passed down from one generation of bakers to the next. This particular recipe makes a lovely pudding cake, which would be delicious served warm with whipped cream or ice cream. It's not a show-stopping cake in terms of looks, but with its nostalgic connections to old-fashioned apple orchards, its popularity will never fade.

fresh apple cake

FOR THE CAKE
1 lemon (unwaxed or well washed)
3–4 apples (you will need about 450–500g small cubes of apple)
225g soft butter, plus extra for greasing
225g light soft brown sugar
3 eggs
230g self-raising flour
1 teaspoon baking powder
½ teaspoon ground cinnamon OR ¼ teaspoon mixed spice (optional)
40g ground almonds
demerara sugar, for sprinkling on top (or use granulated sugar)
cream or ice cream, to serve

YOU WILL NEED
a 23cm springform cake tin, greased with butter and base lined with baking parchment

makes 1 large cake
(serves 8–10)

1/ Preheat the oven to 180°C (gas mark 4).
2/ Finely grate the zest of the lemon into a medium bowl. Add the juice of half the lemon. Peel and core the apples and cut them into small cubes about 1cm square. Add them to the bowl with the lemon zest and juice and toss to coat and prevent browning.
3/ Put the butter and sugar in a large mixing bowl. With a wooden spoon or an electric whisk, cream them together until they are pale and fluffy. Add the eggs one by one, beating well after each addition.
4/ Add the apples, flour, baking powder, cinnamon (if using) and ground almonds, and fold in firmly with a large metal spoon until all the ingredients are well mixed and combined.
5/ Spoon the mixture into the prepared baking tin and smooth the surface with the back of the spoon. Sprinkle a handful of demerara sugar over the surface.
6/ Bake in the preheated oven for 55–60 minutes, checking after 40 minutes to make sure the top is not browning too quickly. If it is, place a double thickness sheet of aluminium foil over the top of the tin. The cake is done when a metal skewer or sharp knife inserted into the center of the cake comes out clean.
7/ Transfer to a wire rack and leave to cool for 10 minutes before releasing from the tin. Serve warm with cream or ice cream. This cake is also good when cold.
STORAGE: Fresh apple cake is best on the day of making, but will keep for 2 days if stored in a cool place. It can be reheated gently in the oven, if preferred.

Streusel is the German word for the topping made with butter, sugar and flour (and often spice and nuts) that is scattered over cakes and pastries to add a layer of crunch and sweetness. It's a finishing touch that has not yet become vintage in the countries where it is popular (Germany, Denmark and Sweden) because it has never gone out of fashion and is still part of a classic baking tradition enjoyed at *Kaffee-und-Küchen* (coffee-and-cake) moments. Fresh, seasonal fruits marry well with streusel toppings and this cake is a good way to use up ripe, juicy plums.

plum streusel

FOR THE CAKE

125g soft butter, plus extra
   for greasing
125g caster sugar
2 eggs
a few drops of vanilla extract (optional)
125g self-raising flour
5–8 fresh plums, pitted and cut
   into quarters
icing sugar, for dusting, if desired
custard, thick cream, whipped cream or
   ice cream, to serve

FOR THE TOPPING

30g cold butter, cubed
60g self-raising flour
a pinch of salt
60g granulated sugar (golden, if you
   have it)
30g hazelnuts, chopped (optional)

YOU WILL NEED

a 20cm round cake tin, greased with butter and base lined with baking parchment

makes 1 large cake
(serves 8–10)

1/ Preheat the oven to 180°C (gas mark 4).
2/ Put the butter and sugar in a large mixing bowl. With a wooden spoon or an electric whisk, cream them together until they are pale and fluffy.
3/ Add the eggs one by one, along with a few drops of vanilla extract (if using), beating well after each addition. Sift over the flour and fold in gently with a large metal spoon.
4/ Spoon the mixture into the prepared tin and smooth the surface with the back of the spoon. Arrange the plum quarters over the top, on their sides and close together in concentric circles.
5/ Make the streusel topping. Put the butter, flour and salt into a mixing bowl. Rub the butter into the flour with your fingertips, until it looks like fine sandy breadcrumbs. Add the granulated sugar and chopped hazelnuts (if using) and stir well to combine. Scatter the streusel topping over the plums.
6/ Bake the cake in the preheated oven for 55–60 minutes until the topping is golden brown, the fruit is bubbling and a metal skewer or sharp knife inserted into the centre of the cake comes out without any uncooked cake mix on it.
7/ Transfer to a wire rack and leave the cake to cool for 15–20 minutes before removing it from the tin.
8/ Dust with icing sugar, if liked. Serve warm with custard, thick cream, whipped cream or ice cream.
STORAGE: This cake is best eaten on the day of making, although it will keep for 1–2 days if wrapped in foil and stored in an airtight tin in a cool place.

This cake has all the makings of a timeless favourite. It's a beguilingly damp, citrussy, almondy cake with an intriguing bite from the polenta. It needs to be eaten with a fork and is best served as a wonderful dessert with something on the side, such as poached apricots, a spoonful of thick, tangy yogurt or crème fraîche, and a glass of something nice, cold and sweet.

polenta cake

FOR THE CAKE

finely grated zest of 3 lemons
(unwaxed or well washed)
juice of ½ a lemon
225g soft butter, plus extra
for greasing
225g caster sugar
3 eggs
200g ground almonds
110g polenta
1 level teaspoon baking powder
a pinch of salt

YOU WILL NEED

a 23cm springform or round loose-bottom cake tin, greased with butter and base lined with baking parchment

*makes 1 medium–large cake
(serves 8–10)*

1/ Preheat the oven to 160°C (gas mark 3).

2/ Start by zesting the 3 lemons, and squeezing one to obtain half its juice. Set aside until needed.

3/ Put the butter and sugar in a large mixing bowl. With a wooden spoon or an electric whisk, cream them together until they are pale and fluffy. Add the eggs one by one, beating well after each addition.

4/ Add the ground almonds, polenta, baking powder, salt and lemon juice and zest. With a large metal spoon or flexible spatula, mix well until all the ingredients are combined. Spoon into the prepared tin and level the surface with the back of the spoon or spatula.

5/ Bake in the preheated oven for 45–50 minutes until the cake is golden brown and pulling away from the sides of the tin and a metal skewer or sharp knife inserted into the centre comes out clean.

6/ Transfer to a wire rack and leave to cool for 10 minutes before turning out of the tin. Serve with creamy yogurt or mascarpone, and a glass of something nice and chilled. Polenta cake is also delicious with a light tea such as Darjeeling.

STORAGE: Polenta cake keeps well for up to 3 days if wrapped in aluminium foil and stored in an airtight tin in a cool place.

Thrifty bakers have known since medieval times that certain naturally sweet vegetables are an economical way of bringing flavour and a long-lasting moist texture to sponge cakes; carrot cake is a widely known example, parsnip cake less so. When paired with pecans and a gentle spice such as nutmeg, parsnips offer a surprisingly subtle flavour which works well with the tangy cream-cheese filling.

parsnip cake

FOR THE CAKE

butter, for greasing
250g parsnips, peeled and grated
75g pecans, chopped (or use walnuts)
250g plain flour
2 teaspoons baking powder
a good grating of nutmeg and a
    generous pinch of mixed spice
1/4 teaspoon salt
250g golden caster sugar
225ml sunflower oil
1 teaspoon vanilla extract
3 eggs

FOR THE FILLING

200g cream cheese
75g soft butter
100g icing sugar
a few drops of vanilla extract

TO FINISH

icing sugar, for dusting

YOU WILL NEED

two 20cm round cake tins, greased with butter and bases lined with baking parchment

makes 1 large cake (serves 10–12)

1/ Preheat the oven to 180°C (gas mark 4).
2/ Prepare the parsnips and pecans, put in a small bowl and set aside until needed. Put the flour, baking powder, spice, salt, sugar, oil and vanilla in a large mixing bowl and beat well with a wooden spoon or an electric whisk until smooth. Add the eggs one by one, beating well after each addition. Add the parsnips and pecans and stir well to mix thoroughly.
3/ Divide the mix equally between the prepared tins. Level the surfaces with the back of the spoon or spatula. Bake in the preheated oven for 20–25 minutes until well risen and golden on top, and a metal skewer or sharp knife inserted into the centre comes out clean. Transfer the cakes to a wire rack and leave to cool for 10–15 minutes before removing from the tins.
4/ When the layers are completely cool, make the filling. Put the cream cheese and butter in a mixing bowl. Sift in the icing sugar and add a few drops of vanilla extract. Mix until smooth with a wooden spoon or flexible spatula. This transformation will happen quite quickly, and the trick with cream-cheese filling is not to overmix.
5/ Put one of the cake layers the wrong way up on a plate or stand, and spread the filling evenly over the surface. Put the other cake layer on top, the right way up, and dust with icing sugar if desired.
STORAGE: Parsnip cake keeps well for 2–3 days if wrapped well in aluminium foil and stored in an airtight tin in a cool place.

maple & walnut cake

Real Canadian maple syrup has a certain unique magic – a combination of its beautiful amber colour, rich caramel aroma and flavour, and concentrated sweetness – which makes it a wonderful ingredient in baking. Beware cheap imitations, though, and use authentic, good-quality syrup combined with soulmate walnuts to create a pale ivory cake suffused with an appealing, gentle toffee sweetness.

maple & walnut cake

FOR THE CAKE

150g soft butter, plus extra
    for greasing
150g light soft brown sugar
3 eggs
4 tablespoons good-quality
    maple syrup
2–3 tablespoons milk
75g walnuts, chopped
220g self-raising flour
16 walnut halves, to decorate

FOR THE TOPPING

200g cream cheese
50g soft butter
80g soft light brown sugar
3–4 tablespoons good-quality
    maple syrup

YOU WILL NEED

a 20cm square cake tin, greased with butter and lined with baking parchment

makes 16 squares

1/ Preheat the oven to 180°C (gas mark 4).

2/ Put the butter and sugar in a large mixing bowl. With a wooden spoon or an electric whisk, cream them together until they are pale and fluffy.

3/ Lightly whisk the eggs and mix with the maple syrup and 2 tablespoons of milk.

4/ Add the liquid ingredients, walnuts and flour to the mixing bowl. With a metal spoon or flexible spatula, fold in gently and thoroughly until the ingredients are well mixed and you have a soft dropping consistency (i.e. the mixture drops off the spoon easily when tapped lightly against the bowl). Add a little more milk if necessary to obtain the right consistency.

5/ Spoon the mixture into the prepared cake tin and level the surface with the back of the spoon. Bake in the preheated oven for 30–35 minutes until well risen and golden brown, and a metal skewer or sharp knife inserted into the centre of the cake comes out clean. Transfer to a wire rack and leave to cool before turning out of the tin. When the cake is completely cool, it is ready for the topping.

6/ To make the topping, put the cream cheese, butter, sugar and 2 tablespoons of maple syrup into a large mixing bowl. With a wooden spoon or an electric whisk, mix well until you have a very smooth and glossy frosting. Add more maple syrup according to taste and to obtain the right consistency.

7/ Spread the frosting in a generous layer to cover the cake. Finish with 16 walnut halves set out in a 4 x 4 grid pattern so that each square will have a walnut half when cut. Just before serving, cut the cake into 16 squares.

STORAGE: Maple and walnut cake is best when fresh, but it will keep well for up to 2 days if wrapped in foil and stored in an airtight tin in a cool place.

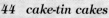

Some cakes are more than just layers of sponge and filling, they are part of our shared baking history. 'Coffee and walnut cake' is shorthand for afternoon tea with vintage bone china cups, leaf tea, a hand-embroidered tablecloth, and polite conversation. The nuts give a nobbly texture to the sponge, while the coffee brings a touch of bitterness to offset the sweet buttercream. It's a cake for sharing; it should be made to good proportions and cut with a relaxed hand to give generous slices.

coffee & walnut cake

FOR THE CAKE

225g soft butter, plus extra
    for greasing
225g light soft brown sugar
4 eggs, lightly beaten
2–4 teaspoons instant coffee
    powder or granules (3 is generally
    the right number)
2 teaspoons boiling water
225g self-raising flour
1½ teaspoons baking powder
65g walnuts, chopped
1 tablespoon milk
8–12 walnut halves for decoration

FOR THE FILLING & TOPPING

400–450g icing sugar (unrefined would
    work very well)
175–200g soft butter
2–3 teaspoons instant coffee powder
    or granules dissolved in 2 teaspoons
    of boiling water

YOU WILL NEED

two 21cm round sandwich tins, greased with butter and lined with greaseproof paper or baking parchment

*makes 1 medium–large cake
(serves 8–10)*

1/ Preheat the oven to 180°C (gas mark 4).

2/ Put the butter and sugar in a large mixing bowl. With a wooden spoon or an electric whisk, cream them together until they are pale and fluffy. Add the eggs one by one, beating well after each addition.

3/ Put the instant coffee and boiling water in a small container (such as an egg cup) and mix until the powder or granules are fully dissolved.

4/ Sift the flour and baking powder into the large bowl containing the butter mixture, pour in the concentrated coffee mix, add the chopped walnuts and the milk and fold together gently with a large metal spoon until thoroughly mixed.

5/ Divide the mixture evenly between the prepared cake tins and bake for 22–25 minutes until the cakes are golden brown and springy, and a metal skewer or sharp knife inserted into the centre of each cake comes out clean.

6/ Leave the cakes on a wire rack to cool for 5 minutes before turning them out of their tins. Leave them to cool completely before filling and icing.

7/ To make the filling and topping: sift 400g of the icing sugar into a bowl and add about 175g of the butter. With a mixer, electric whisk or wooden spoon, beat well until pale and fluffy. Mix the coffee and boiling water as in step 4 and pour into the bowl. Mix again, adding more icing sugar, butter or coffee to taste if necessary until you have a smooth, light, spreadable buttercream. (You can, of course, just use a base of 450g icing sugar and 200g soft butter – this makes a very generous amount of filling and topping.)

8/ Place one of the cake layers upside down on a plate or cake stand. Spread half the buttercream over the surface and place the other layer on top the right way up. Use the remainder of the buttercream to cover the top of the cake. Decorate with walnut halves.

STORAGE: Coffee and walnut cake is at its best on the day of making, but keeps well for a further 1–2 days if stored in an airtight tin in a cool place.

Every home-baker needs a reliable chocolate cake recipe, one that can be made with storecupboard ingredients for parties, cake stalls, gifts and unexpected celebrations. This is the tried-and-tested, vintage Phoebe Brocket recipe that has been used for many years, and never fails to please. Although it's deep and dark in appearance, it is gratifyingly sweet, something which appeals to young and mature palates alike. It's soft and moist enough to serve with cream as a dessert and, as it is large and slices well, it can be dressed up with chocolate sweets and turned into a birthday cake.

simple chocolate cake

FOR THE CAKE
230g soft butter, plus extra
    for greasing
230g caster sugar
4 eggs
180g self-raising flour
50g good-quality cocoa powder
1 level teaspoon baking powder

FOR THE FILLING & TOPPING
350g icing sugar
75g good-quality cocoa powder
100g soft butter
3–4 tablespoons milk, to mix

TO DECORATE
chocolate balls, buttons or other
    chocolate sweets of your choice

YOU WILL NEED
two 20cm round sandwich cake tins,
greased with butter and lined with
baking parchment

*makes 1 medium–large cake
(serves 8–10)*

1/ Preheat the oven to 180°C (gas mark 4).
2/ Put the butter and sugar in a large mixing bowl. With a wooden spoon or an electric whisk, cream them together until they are pale and fluffy. Add the eggs one by one, beating well after each addition.
3/ Measure out the flour, cocoa and baking powder and sift into the bowl. With a large metal spoon, fold in gently and thoroughly until the ingredients are fully combined.
4/ Divide the mixture evenly between the 2 prepared tins, smooth the surfaces with the back of the spoon, and bake in the preheated oven for 20–25 minutes or until a metal skewer or sharp knife inserted into the centre of each cake comes out clean.
5/ Leave the cakes to cool on a wire rack. Remove them from their tins when nearly or completely cool (chocolate cake is crumbly and fragile before it is cold).
6/ Make the chocolate buttercream filling and topping. Sift the icing sugar and cocoa powder into a large bowl and add the butter and 2 tablespoons of milk. Mix well with a round-ended knife or electric whisk, adding more milk if necessary to make the buttercream soft, smooth and easy to spread. Taste and adjust the flavour, adding more icing sugar or cocoa powder if needed, and mix in well.
7/ Place one cake layer upside down on a plate or cake stand. Spread half the buttercream icing on the surface. Place the other cake layer on top, the right way up, and cover the top and sides of the cake with the remaining buttercream. Decorate with chocolate balls, buttons or chocolate sweets of your choice.
STORAGE: Chocolate cake is best on the day of making but it will be fine the next day if you want to make it in advance of an event or occasion.

Carrot cake is well-proportioned, sweetly spiced and utterly reliable, so it's not surprising that it is many a cake-eater's favourite cake. It has been riding a wave of popularity since the 1960s, and despite its ubiquity, it's still a great treat and an ideal celebratory cake. It usually contains cinnamon, although this can be substituted or omitted, but what should never be replaced is the tangy cream-cheese filling to offset all that dense, moist sweetness.

carrot cake

FOR THE CAKES (makes 3 layers)
butter, for greasing
250g plain flour
2 teaspoons baking powder
spice: a good grating of nutmeg and
    a large pinch of mixed spice OR
    1 teaspoon ground cinnamon OR
    1 teaspoon of a mix of ground
    cinnamon, cloves, nutmeg and
    mixed spice
100g walnuts, chopped (or pecans)
250g dark soft brown sugar
220ml sunflower oil (or any mild
    vegetable oil)
3 eggs, lightly beaten
2–3 large carrots (you will need about
    250g grated carrot)

FOR THE FILLING & TOPPING
400g cream cheese
100g soft butter
200g icing sugar

YOU WILL NEED
three 20cm round cake tins, greased
with butter and lined with baking
parchment

*makes 1 large, 3-layer cake
(serves 12–16)*

1/ Preheat the oven to 180°C (gas mark 4).

2/ Sift the flour, baking powder and spice into a bowl. Add the chopped walnuts and stir to mix.

3/ Put the sugar and oil in a large mixing bowl and mix well with a wooden spoon. Now add the beaten eggs and combine well with a wooden spoon or electric whisk until smooth.

4/ Grate the carrots (there is no point in doing this sooner as they start to brown very quickly). Add the carrots, flour and nuts to the mixture in the large bowl. With a large metal spoon or spatula, mix well until thoroughly combined.

5/ Divide the cake mix equally between the 3 cake tins (use electronic scales to be accurate) and level the surfaces with the back of the spoon or spatula. Bake in the preheated oven for 25 minutes until browned and risen, and a metal skewer or sharp knife inserted into the centre of each cake comes out clean. If your oven shelf can accommodate only 2 tins at a time, bake 2 layers first then the final one separately.

6/ Transfer the cakes to a wire rack and leave to cool before turning out of the tins. Carrot cake is quite moist and crumbly and needs to be handled with care.

7/ When all the layers are completely cool, make the cream-cheese filling and assemble the cake. Put the cream cheese and butter in a mixing bowl. Sift in the icing sugar. Mix until smooth with a wooden spoon or flexible spatula. This will happen quite suddenly. Once smooth, do not overmix.

8/ Place a layer of cake upside down on a serving plate or stand. Spread with cream-cheese filling. Repeat with the second layer. Top with the third layer, the right way up, and cover with the filling.

STORAGE: Carrot cake sponge keeps very well for 3–4 days, if you want to make the layers in advance. (It also freezes well.) Wrap well in aluminium foil and store in an airtight tin in a cool place until you are ready to fill and cover the cake. Once filled and covered, the cake is best eaten within 2 days.

Lavender has been prized for its sweet smell since the Tudor era and, as a herb, it has an illustrious culinary history. These days it's both vintage, eau-de-cologne-with-chintz, yet also contemporary fresh and vibrant. Now that good-quality lavender is available to bakers, it can be used to suffuse a sponge cake with its uniquely delicate, aromatic quality. Colouring the icing to match the theme makes the cake a pretty addition to the tea table.

lavender cake

FOR THE CAKE
250g soft butter, plus extra
　　for greasing
250g caster sugar
4 eggs
juice of ½ an orange
1–2 teaspoons culinary dried lavender
　　flower heads
250g self-raising flour
sprig of dried lavender or pale lavender
　　sugar flowers, to decorate

FOR THE FILLING & TOPPING
100g soft butter
400g icing sugar
3–5 tablespoons orange juice OR milk
　　(Note: If you are using lavender
　　extract to flavour the buttercream,
　　use milk instead of orange juice)
a few drops of culinary lavender extract
a small amount of purple food colouring
　　paste – Sugarflair 'Grape Violet'
　　gives a nice shade of lavender
　　(optional)

YOU WILL NEED
two 21cm round loose-bottomed
sandwich tins, greased and bases lined
with baking parchment

*makes 1 medium–large cake
(serves 8–10)*

1/ Preheat the oven to 180°C (gas mark 4).

2/ Put the butter and sugar in a large mixing bowl. With a wooden spoon or an electric whisk, cream them together until they are pale and fluffy. Add the eggs one by one, beating well after each addition.

3/ Add the orange juice, lavender heads and self-raising flour. Fold in gently with a large metal spoon until well combined.

4/ Divide the mixture evenly between the 2 sandwich tins (use electronic scales for accuracy). Smooth the surfaces with the back of the spoon. Bake in the preheated oven for 23–25 minutes until golden brown and springy to the touch, and a metal skewer or sharp knife inserted into the centre of each cake comes out clean. Transfer to a wire rack and leave to cool for a few minutes before turning out of the tins.

5/ When cool, make the filling and topping. Put the butter in a large mixing bowl, and sift in the icing sugar. Add 2 tablespoons of orange juice OR milk plus the lavender extract (if using), and mix well either with an electric whisk or a large knife until the mixture is smooth, fluffy and has changed to a very pale colour. Gradually add more liquid to give a soft, spreadable consistency.

6/ Add the colouring (if using) when you have the right consistency, but not before. When you are ready to colour, add a small amount of paste at a time (on the end of a cocktail stick) until you have the depth of colour you like.

7/ To assemble the cake: place a layer upside down on the serving plate so that you have a flat surface to ice. If necessary, carefully slice off any roundness on the top so that it sits flat on the plate. With a palette knife or round-ended knife, spread half the buttercream over the bottom layer, then add the top layer, the right way up. Without pressing down too much, spread the remainder of the topping over the surface of the cake. Decorate with a little sprig of fresh lavender or a few sugar flowers.

STORAGE: Lavender cake is best eaten on the day of making, but will keep for a day or two longer if stored in an airtight tin in a cool place.

Every baker needs a collection of tried-and-tested recipes for quick and easy, simple and homely cakes that can be whipped up at a moment's notice. Keep your eggs and butter on stand-by, and you will always be ready to create reassuringly old-fashioned treats that fill your kitchen with warmth and good smells, and give pleasure to everyone. This chapter includes many classic everyday cakes that have been enjoyed by generations of hungry, school-tired children, and by friends popping in for elevenses for a restorative pot of tea and a chat. They are part of a tradition of generosity and thoughtfulness, a tradition that is worth sustaining. It is always useful having a couple of speedy recipes that can be made without fuss with storecupboard ingredients just before people arrive. These days there are so many excuses for a quick bake – from hosting book groups and crafty get-togethers, to cheering up cold winter afternoons and teaching children how to measure and mix – that we should embrace our baking heritage at every opportunity and cake whim.

everyday
cakes

The Victoria sandwich cake would probably top most people's list of fondly remembered vintage cakes. It's been around since Queen Victoria herself and is as delicious as it is simple. It's light, buttery and very moreish, especially when filled with whipped cream and red jam, although many claim it needs only the jam to make it a classic Victoria sandwich.

victoria sandwich cake

FOR THE CAKE

180g soft butter, plus extra
    for greasing
180g caster sugar
3 eggs, lightly beaten
½ teaspoon good-quality vanilla
    extract (optional)
180g self-raising flour
1–2 tablespoons whole milk

FOR THE FILLING

about 4 tablespoons raspberry jam (or
    any jam you like)
about 250ml double or whipping cream
icing sugar, for dusting

YOU WILL NEED

two 18cm round loose-bottomed cake
tins, greased with butter and bases
lined with baking parchment

makes 1 medium cake
(serves 8)

1/ Preheat the oven to 180°C (gas mark 4).
2/ Put the butter and sugar in a large mixing bowl. With a wooden spoon or an electric whisk cream them together until they are very pale and fluffy. Allow at least 2 minutes with an electric whisk for this, more if you are mixing by hand. Every so often, scrape down the sides with a flexible spatula to ensure everything is evenly mixed.
3/ Add the beaten eggs one by one and the vanilla extract (if using), mixing well after each addition, until the mixture is very pale and fluffy. Sift the flour into the bowl. Using a large metal spoon, very gently fold in the flour, adding a tablespoon of milk, or more if needed, to give a light, smooth consistency.
4/ Divide the mixture equally between the 2 prepared tins (use electronic scales for accuracy). Smooth the surfaces with the back of the spoon.
5/ Bake in the middle of the preheated oven for 20–25 minutes. The cakes are ready when they are firm to the touch, are pulling away from the sides and a metal skewer or sharp knife inserted into the centre of each cake comes out clean. Transfer to a wire rack and leave to cool for a few minutes before turning out of the tins. Leave to cool completely before filling.
6/ Place a layer of sponge upside down on a plate or cake stand and cover with a generous layer of your chosen jam. Whip the cream until it forms soft peaks – overwhipping spoils the texture – and spread a layer over the jam. Place the other layer on top, the right way up, and dust with icing sugar by putting a very small amount in a sieve and gently shaking it above the cake.
STORAGE: The sponge layers can be made in advance, preferably on the day of eating. Once filled the cake should be enjoyed straightaway.

variation

For a delicious and impressive-looking summer cake, replace the jam with fresh strawberries (raspberries would work equally well). Fill the cake with a layer of whipped cream then a generous scattering of strawberries, and decorate the top of the cake with more whipped cream and strawberries.

Scones are quick and easy to make, and although they are associated with dainty afternoon events and generous cream teas, you don't have to have a special reason for making a batch. Any excuse will do to rustle up a tray of airy, lightly sweet scones to act as vehicles for a lavish amount of jam and cream. Put the kettle on, make a pot of tea, sit down and enjoy them at their best: fresh out of the oven.

scones

FOR THE SCONES

500g self-raising flour, plus extra
    for dusting
½ teaspoon salt
100g cold butter, cubed
100g caster sugar
80–100g sultanas or to taste (optional)
2 eggs
about 250ml milk
clotted cream, whipped cream,
    butter, jam or honey, to serve

YOU WILL NEED

2 baking sheets, lined with greaseproof
    paper or baking parchment
a 5cm round cutter

makes 20–22 scones

cook's tips

Halve the recipe quantities if you are baking for just a few people.

If you don't have a cutter to hand, make square scones. Form the dough into a square with your hands and cut into squares with a sharp knife.

1/ Preheat the oven to 200°C (gas mark 6).

2/ Sift the flour and salt into a large mixing bowl. With your fingertips, rub the butter into the flour until it resembles very fine breadcrumbs. Add the sugar and sultanas (if using) and stir gently to mix.

3/ Put the eggs and 150ml of the milk in a small bowl or jug and mix well with a fork. Make a well in the centre of the dry mixture in the bowl and pour in the egg and milk mix. Working quickly with a fork or ordinary knife, bring the ingredients together to make a damp, soft, but not too sticky dough. Carefully add more milk in small quantities if necessary if the dough feels too dry and crumbly.

4/ With your hands, form the dough into a thick disc and place on a floured work surface. With a rolling pin or just using your hands, flatten or roll out quickly and gently to about 3cm thick.

5/ Using a 5cm round cutter, cut out as many rounds as possible, placing them in rows, a few inches apart, on the prepared baking sheets. Re-form the leftovers into a flat disc, roll out again and cut more rounds. Repeat until all the dough has been used. Brush the tops with milk to make a light glaze.

6/ Bake, in batches if necessary, in the preheated oven for 10–15 minutes until well risen and golden but not brown on top. Smaller scones will cook faster than large scones, so if yours are larger than 5cm, add on extra time. The same applies if you decide to make square scones (see tip opposite).

7/ Transfer to a wire rack and leave the scones to cool for 5 minutes. Serve very fresh with your chosen accompaniments.

STORAGE: Scones are at their very best when fresh, although they can be baked a morning or day in advance if necessary. Store in an airtight tin in a cool place.

variation

Scones can be plain or fruited, and fruit added or omitted according to taste. Sultanas are the classic scone fruit, but they can be replaced with dried sour cherries or chopped dried apricots as you prefer.

These small, fruity cakes conjure up images of old-fashioned flat heavy pans on open fires in stone cottages in Wales. Welsh cakes have a very cosy, comforting, fireside feel and are excellent for dark afternoons when it is wet and windy outside. You can be eating them very soon after thinking about them as they can be put together in a matter of minutes, and are best eaten straightaway, although they will keep until the next day if you want to send someone off to school or work with a bundle. Welsh miners used to carry them in their pockets when they went down the coal mines so they are also sometimes known as Welsh miners' cakes.

welsh cakes

FOR THE CAKES

225g self-raising flour,
   plus extra for dusting
a pinch of salt
100g cold butter, cubed
75g caster sugar, plus extra
   for sprinkling
75g currants or whatever dried fruit
   is to hand, such as mixed dried fruit,
   raisins or sultanas
1 egg
2 tablespoons milk

YOU WILL NEED

a 6cm round cookie cutter and
a griddle or flat, heavy-based pan

*makes 18
cakes*

1/ Sift the flour and salt into a mixing bowl. Add the small cubes of cold butter and rub into the flour with your fingertips, until it looks like fine breadcrumbs. Add the sugar and dried fruit and stir to mix and distribute.

2/ With a fork, mix the egg with the milk in a separate small bowl. Add to the mixing bowl and with a round-ended knife or your hands, bring the ingredients together to make a soft, damp, but not sticky dough. If it is too dry and won't come together, add a few more drops of milk, bearing in mind that this is a buttery dough which will become softer and stickier as you handle it with warm hands.

3/ Turn the dough onto a lightly floured surface. With a rolling pin, roll out to about 1cm thick. Cut out 6cm rounds using the cutter, re-rolling the trimmings as necessary to make more rounds.

4/ Heat the griddle or pan over a medium heat. Grease very lightly if necessary; do this by putting a dab of butter on a piece of kitchen paper and wiping the surface of the griddle while hot, using the paper to pick up any residue butter. Welsh cakes should not be fried and many cooks don't grease the griddle at all.

5/ Cook the cakes in batches for 3 minutes on each side, until they are puffed up and a deep golden brown on top. Take care not to burn by cooking them over too high a heat. Remove the cakes from the griddle, sprinkle with sugar and eat straightaway.

STORAGE: See cook's tip below (although they can be eaten the next day if stored in an airtight tin).

cook's tip

*Welsh cakes do not keep well,
and are at their best when
eaten as soon as they have
been made.*

Real sweet muffins made at home to vintage recipes and enjoyed when fresh and warm are one of life's great fast foods. They are quick and easy to put together for breakfast or brunch, and are light years away from the oversized, sweet, spongy, long-lasting muffins sold in supermarkets. Traditional muffins are low in sugar, but because they contain a large proportion of baking powder, they are high in airiness and texture. Serve immediately with jam or honey, coffee or juice, or wrap in paper and take to work or school.

muffins

FOR THE MUFFINS
2 oranges (unwaxed or well washed)
6 teaspoons clear, runny honey
80g butter
300g plain flour
1 tablespoon baking powder
1 teaspoon salt
75g oatmeal
100g caster sugar
150ml milk
2 eggs, lightly beaten

YOU WILL NEED
a 12-hole muffin tin, greased
with butter

makes 12–15 large muffins

upside-down orange & honey muffins

1/ Preheat the oven to 180°C (gas mark 4).
2/ Start by preparing the oranges. Finely grate the zest of 1 orange and set aside on a small plate until later. With a sharp knife, carefully peel each orange, removing all peel and pith until you have just the fruit showing. Cut the oranges into slices about 5mm thick. Remove any pips. An orange should give about 6–8 slices.
3/ Place half a teaspoonful of honey in the base of each muffin hole, and place a slice of orange in each one. You may need to trim the slices to fit.
4/ Now make the muffin batter. In a small saucepan, heat the butter until just melted. Set aside to cool.
5/ Put the flour, baking powder, salt, oatmeal, sugar and reserved orange zest into a large mixing bowl and mix with a fork to distribute the ingredients evenly.
6/ Measure the milk in a measuring jug. Add the lightly beaten egg and the melted butter, and mix well with a fork or small whisk until thoroughly combined.
7/ Pour the liquid onto the dry ingredients and quickly stir with a wooden spoon or flexible spatula until just combined. Do not overwork the mixture.
8/ Spoon the mix over the orange slices in the muffin tin, filling each hole about two-thirds full. Bake in the preheated oven for 18–20 minutes, or until the tops are golden brown and springy to the touch, and a metal skewer or sharp knife inserted into the centre of a muffin comes out clean.
9/ Transfer to a wire rack and leave to cool for a couple of minutes. To turn the muffins out of the tin, turn the tin over swiftly in one movement to allow the muffins to slide out onto the cooling rack. Give the tin a gentle shake to dislodge any that are sticking. Do not leave the muffins too long before turning them out as they can become very sticky and difficult to remove.
10/ Serve these muffins upside down so the orange slices can be seen and admired. The muffins are best served warm (but not immediately as hot honey can burn mouths) with butter and/or marmalade, or simply on their own.
STORAGE: Eat on the same day, within a couple of hours of baking as these muffins do not keep well.

sour cherry muffins

FOR THE MUFFINS

100g dried sour cherries

finely grated zest of 1 orange (unwaxed or well washed)

2–3 tablespoons gin or fresh orange juice

60g butter, plus extra for greasing

280g plain flour

1 tablespoon baking powder

½ teaspoon salt

70g caster sugar

150ml milk

1 egg, lightly beaten

YOU WILL NEED

a 12-hole muffin tin, greased with butter or lined with paper muffin cases

makes 12 large muffins

cook's tip

When you are ready to bake, make sure you have all the ingredients measured out and ready before you start mixing. When making muffins, speed is of the essence once you mix wet with dry ingredients.

sour cherry muffins

1/ Start these muffins the night before they are needed. Put the dried cherries in a small bowl, add the orange zest and pour over the gin or orange juice. Stir to mix. Cover and leave in the fridge overnight until you are ready to bake. (If you forget to start the night before, just mix the cherries and gin or juice and carry on. The cherries won't be as plump, but they will still taste good.)

2/ Preheat the oven to 180°C (gas mark 4).

3/ In a small saucepan, heat the butter until just melted. Set aside to cool. In a large mixing bowl, combine the flour, baking powder, salt and sugar, and stir to mix. Measure the milk in a measuring jug. Add the lightly beaten egg and the melted butter, and mix well with a fork or small whisk until thoroughly combined.

4/ Pour the liquid ingredients onto the dry ingredients. Add the soaked cherries and their syrupy liquid. Stir with a wooden spoon or flexible spatula until just combined – do not overwork the mixture.

5/ Spoon the mix into the muffin tin, filling each paper case two-thirds full. Bake in the preheated oven for 18–20 minutes, or until the tops are golden brown and springy to the touch, and a metal skewer or sharp knife inserted into the centre of a muffin comes out clean.

6/ Transfer to a wire rack, leave to cool for a few minutes and then remove the muffins from the tin. These muffins are delicious eaten warm with butter and/or morello cherry jam.

STORAGE: Eat within a few hours of baking.

No official history exists for this ultra-rich, addictively sweet 'fridge cake', although it is hard to overlook the connection to 'tiffin', the name for a light meal or a between-meal snack in India. For generations of thrifty bakers, tiffin was a way of using up broken biscuits left at the bottom of the tin and any of the leftover dried fruits lurking in the larder. These days it's often made with ever-more expensive and exotic ingredients, but the fact remains that plain, old-fashioned, economical tiffin is a great treat and a delicious taste of the past.

chocolate tiffin

FOR THE CAKE

100g butter, plus extra for greasing
2 tablespoons cocoa powder
2 tablespoons golden syrup
200g digestive biscuits
150g raisins and 100g undyed glacé cherries (rinsed and halved)
  OR a total of 250g of your chosen fruits which could also include sultanas, dried sour cherries, blueberries, apricots, pear, candied peel or ginger, coconut, or chopped nuts such as pistachios, pecans or hazelnuts
200g good-quality milk chocolate

YOU WILL NEED

a 20cm square cake tin, greased with butter and lined with baking parchment

makes 16 squares

1/ Put the butter, cocoa powder and golden syrup in a large, solid saucepan. Warm gently over a low heat until the ingredients have melted, stirring frequently to combine. Set aside.

2/ Crush the digestives into fine crumbs. The easiest way is to put them in a sealable plastic bag, place the bag on a hard surface (such as the floor) and crush with a rolling pin or your bare or stockinged feet.

3/ Add the dried fruit and the biscuit crumbs to the saucepan and mix well with a wooden spoon or flexible spatula until everything is combined and well covered.

4/ Tip the mixture into the prepared tin and press down with the back of a metal spoon or the palm of your hand to give a smooth surface, making sure the corners are filled. Cover with clingfilm and put in the fridge to start cooling while you melt the chocolate.

5/ Break the chocolate into pieces and put it in a heatproof bowl over a pan of just-boiled water (the water should come about two-thirds up the side of the bowl). Take care not to get any water in the chocolate. Leave for a few minutes to melt, stirring only occasionally.

6/ Pour the melted chocolate over the cooled mixture in the tin, shaking and tipping it gently to ensure the chocolate covers the surface evenly.

7/ Return the tin to the fridge to cool for at least 2 hours before eating, or overnight if possible.

STORAGE: Chocolate tiffin keeps for several days in the fridge, but melts quickly once it is taken out.

Genoa cake needs to be rescued from its plastic wrapping and replaced where it belongs: in the canon of favourite vintage cakes. For too long it has been associated with slabs of cake, sliced to display the fruit content, sold in garden centres and farm shops, when in fact it is at its best when baked at home. The name may very well come from an association with the Genoese fruit bread, or *pandolce*, which is made with plenty of sultanas, and is less dense and dry than other traditional, festive Italian cakes. The Genoa cake that was so popular in Victorian times was, and still is, suitably light, soft and crumbly, and has a crunchy topping of demerara sugar. This is a family-friendly cake that keeps well and is perfect for tea-breaks.

genoa cake

FOR THE CAKE
250g sultanas
150g glacé cherries, washed and halved
75g mixed peel
50g flaked almonds
grated zest of 1 lemon
2 tablespoons rum or brandy
230g soft butter, plus extra for greasing
230g caster sugar (unrefined is preferable)
4 eggs
320g self-raising flour
demerara sugar, for sprinkling

YOU WILL NEED
a 20cm round cake tin, greased with butter and lined with baking parchment

makes 1 large cake (serves 10)

1/ Preheat the oven to 160°C (gas mark 3).
2/ Measure out the fruits and flaked almonds into a small bowl. Add the grated lemon zest and rum or brandy. Stir to mix. Set aside until needed.
3/ Put the butter and sugar in a large mixing bowl. With a wooden spoon or an electric whisk, cream them together until they are pale and fluffy. Add the eggs one by one, beating well after each addition.
4/ Add the flour and the fruit and nut mix. Fold in gently and thoroughly with a large metal spoon. Spoon into the prepared cake tin and level the surface with the back of the spoon. Sprinkle generously with demerara sugar.
5/ Bake for 1½–1¾ hours until the surface is golden brown and slightly cracked, and a metal skewer or sharp knife inserted into the centre of the cake comes out clean. Transfer to a wire rack and leave to cool before turning out of the tin.

STORAGE: Genoa cake keeps well for 4–5 days if wrapped in greaseproof paper or foil and stored in an airtight tin in a cool place.

Despite their many associations with North America, in fact no single country or region of the world can lay claim to inventing doughnuts. The practice of deep-frying a ball or ring of dough in hot fat is as historically long as it is geographically widespread. However, in popular culture and imagination, the doughnut's spiritual home is the USA, although it's possible to argue that its holiday home is firmly established in the traditional British seaside town. Crisp and chewy on the outside, soft and yielding on the inside, with perhaps a smooth, runny, jammy centre and a crunchy, sugary topping, doughnuts offer a festival of texture.

doughnuts

FOR THE DOUGHNUTS

1 x 7g sachet fast-action yeast or
    1 1/2 teaspoons dried yeast
1 teaspoon sugar
250ml milk
500g strong plain flour, plus extra
    for dusting
1 teaspoon salt
50g butter
50g caster sugar
1 egg (if halving the quantities,
    still use 1 egg)

TO FINISH

200g white or golden caster sugar
2 tablespoons seedless raspberry jam
    (or raspberry jam warmed then
    strained to remove lumps and pips)
    if making jam-filled doughnuts

YOU WILL NEED

a large, deep, solid saucepan, one-third
    full of light vegetable or sunflower
    oil for deep-frying
a sugar thermometer
a kitchen syringe or piping bag with
    long thin nozzle
2 baking sheets lined with baking
    parchment
kitchen paper

makes 16–24 doughnuts
(depending on size)

1/ Start by making the yeast starter following the instructions on page 17. Put the remaining 400g flour and the salt in a large mixing bowl. Add the butter and rub into the flour with your fingertips until it resembles very fine breadcrumbs. Add the sugar and stir to mix.

2/ Pour the yeast starter onto the flour, add the egg, and with your hand, bring the ingredients together into a soft, rough dough. Turn out onto a floured work surface and knead for 4–5 minutes until the dough is smooth and pliable. Form into a ball. Lightly oil the mixing bowl and return the dough to the bowl. Roll the ball round the bowl to ensure it picks up a very light coating of oil. Cover the bowl with clingfilm and leave to rise in a warm, draught-free place for 1 1/2–2 hours or until doubled in size (the time taken depends on the room temperature).

3/ With floured hands, punch down the dough and turn it out onto a lightly floured work surface. Knead for a minute until all the air has been knocked out. Divide the dough into as many doughnuts as you wish to make, bearing in mind that each doughnut will expand to double its size. Shape into balls or rings and place the doughnuts well apart on a baking sheet. Cover with oiled clingfilm and leave to rise again for 45 minutes. Put the sugar into a wide-bottomed bowl ready to cover the doughnuts.

4/ Towards the end of the rising, heat the oil in the pan to 180–190°C. If you don't have a thermometer, test the temperature by dropping in a small cube of bread – if it turns golden brown within a minute, the oil is hot enough. Fry 2–3 doughnuts at a time, gently lowering them into the fat on a slotted spoon. Exact cooking times will vary according to the size of the doughnuts, but generally it takes 2–3 minutes on each side. Check the temperature of the oil after each batch.

5/ Remove each doughnut carefully with a slotted spoon and transfer to a plate covered with kitchen paper. Leave to drain for 30 seconds, then toss in the caster sugar. If you prefer a lighter coating, simply sift caster sugar over the doughnuts.

6/ If filling with jam, spoon the jam into the syringe and inject into the side of the doughnut. If using a piping bag, make a small hole in the side with a skewer, press the nozzle in and squeeze jam inside.

STORAGE: They are at their best when still warm and fresh on the day of making.

The legendary John Tovey of the Miller Howe Hotel in the Lake District is credited with creating this wildly popular pudding cake in the 1970s. There is nothing minimal about it; it's a marriage of dark sponge, sticky dates and toffee sauce that could have been made in heaven if it hadn't been thought up in a kitchen next to a lake. It has since become a feature of many a restaurant menu, although it's a brilliant recipe to make at home – a truly comforting pudding that is much lighter than you might imagine. If you want to, you can double the quantity of sauce and really indulge.

sticky toffee pudding cake

FOR THE CAKE

150g medjool dates (pitted weight)
220ml boiling water
80g soft butter, plus extra for greasing
130g light soft brown sugar or light muscovado sugar
2 eggs
1 teaspoon vanilla extract
2 tablespoons golden syrup
2 teaspoons bicarbonate of soda
200g plain flour
double or whipped cream (optional), to serve

FOR THE SAUCE

100g dark muscovado sugar or dark soft brown sugar
100g butter
150ml double cream

YOU WILL NEED

a 20cm square baking tin, greased with butter and base lined with baking parchment

*makes 1 large cake
(serves 8–10 as a pudding)*

1/ Preheat the oven to 180°C (gas mark 4).

2/ Chop the dates and put them in a small bowl. Pour over the boiling water and leave to stand for a few minutes.

3/ Put the butter and sugar in a large mixing bowl. With a wooden spoon or an electric whisk, cream them together until they are pale and fluffy. Add the eggs one by one, beating well after each addition. Add the vanilla extract and the golden syrup (this is much easier if you first heat the tablespoon by holding it in or under very hot water, then dry it before quickly using it). Stir to mix.

4/ Add the bicarbonate of soda to the dates and water and stir briefly to mix (it will foam very quickly).

5/ Add the flour to the mixing bowl, then the dates and water. With a large metal spoon or flexible spatula, mix the ingredients, stirring well to make a smooth, runny batter.

6/ Pour into the prepared tin. Bake in the preheated oven for 35–40 minutes until well risen and deep brown, and a metal skewer or sharp knife inserted into the centre comes out clean.

7/ While the cake is baking, make the sauce. Put all the sauce ingredients into a small saucepan. Heat gently until the butter has melted, stirring frequently. Continue until you have a smooth, translucent sauce. Remove from the heat and set aside.

8/ When the cake is ready to come out of the oven, transfer to a wire rack and leave for a few minutes before turning out of the tin. If you are serving the cake immediately, pour some of the sauce over the still-hot cake and cut into squares. Serve with the remaining sauce and cream (if using). If you are making this ahead of time, leave the cake in the tin and pour some of the sauce over it while still hot. Reheat the cake until just warm in a low oven (if you aim to make it piping hot, it will dry out). Reheat the sauce, and serve.

STORAGE: Sticky toffee pudding cake is best fresh, but it can be frozen successfully. The sauce should be made on the day of serving.

Although this is baked in a loaf tin, it's not a true bread as it uses baking powder and bicarbonate of soda as fast-acting raising agents. Such 'breads' were popular in America long before they travelled abroad, but such is their ease of making, reliability and low cost, they have now become part of the vintage cake repertoire all over the world. Banana bread is a classic – a stalwart of the tea table, lunchboxes, picnics and cake tins, as it keeps well and slices beautifully. It's a wonderful way of using up overripe bananas (it's worth ripening a couple deliberately) and a cheap way of filling your kitchen with delicious aromas.

banana bread

FOR THE CAKE

150g soft butter, plus extra for
    greasing
270g light soft brown sugar
2 eggs
200g very ripe banana (about
    2 bananas in peeled weight)
a squeeze of lemon juice
1 teaspoon vanilla extract
280g plain flour
1 level teaspoon bicarbonate of soda
1 level teaspoon baking powder
a pinch of salt
optional spice: ½ teaspoon cinnamon/
    mixed spice/ginger or grated
    nutmeg, to taste

YOU WILL NEED

a loaf tin, about 23 x 13 x 7cm,
greased with butter OR 12–14 mini
metal loaf tins, greased with butter
OR 12–14 mini disposable cardboard
loaf cases

*makes 1 large loaf OR
12–14 mini loaves*

1/ Preheat the oven to 180°C (gas mark 4).

2/ Put the butter and sugar in a large mixing bowl. With a wooden spoon or an electric whisk, cream them together until they are pale and fluffy. Add the eggs one by one, beating well after each addition.

3/ Put the peeled bananas in a small bowl and add a good squeeze of lemon juice. Mash well with a fork. Add the vanilla extract and mix in. Add this to the butter and sugar mixture and combine well.

4/ Measure out the flour, bicarbonate of soda, baking powder, salt and any spices (if using) in a small bowl, then sift them into the large bowl. With a metal spoon or flexible spatula, mix gently but firmly until the ingredients are fully combined.

5/ Pour into the prepared loaf tin, or spoon into the individual tins or loaf cases, filling each one just over half full. Bake in the preheated oven for 1 hour if making a large loaf or for 20–25 minutes if making small loaves. The banana bread is done when a metal skewer or sharp knife inserted into the centre comes out clean.

6/ Transfer to a wire rack and leave to cool. If using metal tins, turn the loaves out when cool. If using disposable loaf cases, leave inside.

STORAGE: Banana bread is delicious warm from the oven, but keeps well for a couple of days if wrapped and stored in a cool place.

Looking through the list of ingredients for tea loaf (which is very similar to the vintage Welsh *bara brith*), you would be forgiven for thinking this recipe must turn out extremely plain and dull. But you would be wrong. Although it's one of the most straightforward and economical cakes of all, it has a lovely texture and taste, slices beautifully and is delicious spread with butter and served with hot tea. It has been baked by many generations of frugal bakers, and is often associated with church or chapel high teas and funeral teas as it's tasty and comforting, and doesn't contain any alcohol. Ordinary tea is used for soaking the fruit, but you could experiment with more aromatic varieties such as Earl Grey or Lapsang Souchong.

tea loaf

FOR THE LOAF

375g mixed dried fruit and peel
250ml strained, cold tea (strong, no
    milk or sugar)
butter, for greasing
150g soft brown sugar or muscovado
    sugar (dark or light)
1 egg, lightly beaten
250g plain flour
1 heaped teaspoon baking powder
a pinch of mixed spice, grated nutmeg
    or ground cloves (optional)
grated zest of 1 lemon

YOU WILL NEED

a loaf tin, about 22 x 11 x 7cm,
greased with butter and lined with
baking parchment.

makes 1 large loaf
(serves 8–10)

1/ Begin the night before. Put the dried fruit and cold tea in a mixing bowl. Cover and leave to soak overnight at room temperature.

2/ Next day, when you are ready to bake, preheat the oven to 160°C (gas mark 3), and grease and line the loaf tin.

3/ Add the sugar and egg to the soaked fruit and mix well with a wooden spoon or flexible spatula. Sift in the flour, baking powder and spice (if using), and mix well until thoroughly combined.

4/ Spoon the mixture into the prepared loaf tin and level the surface with the back of the spoon. Bake in the centre of the oven for 1–1¼ hours until a metal skewer or sharp knife inserted into the centre of the cake comes out clean.

5/ Transfer to a wire rack, and allow to cool before turning out of the tin. Serve in slices, with butter as an option.

STORAGE: Tea loaf keeps well for 2–3 days if wrapped in foil and stored in an airtight tin.

In days gone by, when cakes were plainer and simpler, Madeira cake was the ultimate in plain, simple, yet very good baking. Despite the name, the ingredients do not include Madeira. Rather, it was a cake that could be served mid-morning or mid-afternoon with a small glass of the sweet, fortified wine. The crack along the top of the cake is deliberate, and part of the distinctive appearance which suggests, correctly, lots of lovely butter and eggs. Old recipes suggest placing two long strips of candied lemon peel along the top of the cake midway through baking, which makes a delightful finishing touch.

madeira cake

FOR THE CAKE

175g soft butter, plus extra
    for greasing
175g caster sugar
250g plain flour
3/4 teaspoon baking powder
finely grated zest of 1/2 a lemon
4 eggs
2 strips of candied lemon peel,
    to decorate (optional)

YOU WILL NEED

a loaf tin, about 24 x 14 x 7cm,
greased with butter and lined with
baking parchment

*makes 1 medium cake
(serves 8–10)*

1/ Preheat the oven to 160°C (gas mark 3).

2/ Put the butter and sugar in a large mixing bowl. With a wooden spoon or an electric whisk, cream them together until they are pale and fluffy.

3/ Sift the flour and baking powder into a small bowl. Add the lemon zest.

4/ Add the eggs to the butter and sugar mixture one by one, beating well after each addition. If the mixture splits (curdles), add a small amount of flour and carry on beating. When all the eggs have been incorporated, add the flour mix. With a large metal spoon, fold in well until all the ingredients are thoroughly combined. Spoon into the prepared tin and smooth the surface with the back of the spoon.

5/ Bake in the preheated oven for 55–60 minutes until well risen and firm to the touch, and a metal skewer or sharp knife inserted into the centre of the cake comes out clean. If you are using the strips of peel, place them along the centre of the cake after 40 minutes and continue baking. Transfer to a wire rack and leave to cool for 15 minutes before turning out of the tin.

STORAGE: Madeira cake doesn't necessarily need any accompaniment and is at its best when fresh and still faintly warm, but it will keep, wrapped in foil and stored in a cool place, for a couple of days.

One of the most appealing aspects of Swedish life is the culture of coffee and cake, enjoyed in welcoming, warm cafés which are havens of plain, simple, but very tasty baking. Swedish tosca cake is one of the country's best-loved cakes, enjoyed for its contrasting soft sweetness and nutty crunchiness. It's typically Scandinavian: relaxed yet stylish, and well worth adopting.

swedish tosca cake

FOR THE CAKE

4 eggs
200g caster sugar
200ml double cream
110g butter, melted then cooled,
    plus extra for greasing
2 teaspoons vanilla extract
250g plain flour
2 teaspoons baking powder
cream, softly whipped, to serve

FOR THE TOPPING

75g butter
75g caster sugar
50ml double cream
30g plain flour
100g flaked almonds

YOU WILL NEED

a 25cm round loose-bottomed or springform cake tin, greased with butter and lined with baking parchment

*makes 1 very large cake
(serves 12–16)*

1/ Preheat the oven to 200°C (gas mark 6).

2/ Put the eggs and sugar into a large mixing bowl and mix for 8 minutes until pale, thick and creamy. Add the cream, melted butter and vanilla extract and fold in very gently with a large metal spoon.

3/ Sift in the flour and baking powder, and continue to fold in until all the ingredients are thoroughly combined.

4/ Pour the mixture into the prepared cake tin and gently level the surface with the back of the spoon. Put the cake in the preheated oven and set the timer for 30 minutes.

5/ While the cake is baking, make the topping. Put all of the topping ingredients into a saucepan and, stirring frequently, heat gently until the butter has melted and the ingredients are fully mixed.

6/ After 30 minutes' baking, remove the cake from the oven or simply open the door and pull the rack out towards you so that you can spread the Tosca topping over the cake and then return it quickly to the oven. Continue to bake for a further 10–15 minutes or until the top is golden brown and lightly caramelised. Serve with softly whipped cream.

STORAGE: Swedish tosca cake is best on the day of making, but will keep for a couple of days if wrapped in foil and stored in an airtight tin in a cool place.

Lard gets a bad press these days, yet it is part of a long and proud baking heritage (many pastry-makers still swear by its lightness). Lardy cake is a very rich and sweet layered bread into which as much lard, sugar and dried fruit as possible is crammed. It is unashamedly calorific, an energy booster for tired workers and schoolchildren, a treat on high days and holidays. It may seem old-fashioned, but it remains popular in country town and village bakeries, and has even been served at Buckingham Palace garden parties. (You could substitute the lard with butter, but the result wouldn't be true lardy cake.)

lardy cake

FOR THE CAKE

1 x 7g sachet fast-action yeast or
   1 dessertspoon dried yeast
1 teaspoon sugar
250ml milk (more if necessary)
500g strong white flour, plus extra
   for dusting
1 teaspoon salt
175g lard (or half and half lard
   and butter)
175g light soft brown sugar or light
   muscovado sugar
225g mixed dried fruit
caster sugar, for sprinkling

YOU WILL NEED

1 baking sheet, lined with baking
parchment

*makes 1 large cake
(about 16 squares)*

1/ Make a yeast starter following the instructions on page 17. Put the remaining 400g flour and the salt in a large mixing bowl. Add the yeast liquid and with your hand bring the ingredients together into a soft, lightly sticky dough, adding more milk if necessary to get a soft consistency that will be easy to knead.

2/ Turn out onto a floured work surface and knead for 4–5 minutes until the dough is smooth and pliable, and starts to feel slightly clammy. Form into a ball. Lightly oil the mixing bowl (no need to wash before doing this) and return the dough to the bowl. Roll the ball round the bowl to ensure it picks up a very light coating of oil. Cover the bowl with clingfilm and leave to rise in a warm, draught-free place for 1½–2 hours until doubled in size (the time taken depends on the room temperature).

3/ Prepare the remaining ingredients. Cut the lard into small cubes. Toss the sugar and dried fruit together in a small bowl.

4/ With a floured hand, knock back the dough and turn out onto a floured work surface. Roll out into a large rectangle just under 1cm thick. Sprinkle two-thirds of the dough with one-third of the fruit and sugar mix and dot a third of the lard cubes over the top. Now lift up the uncovered third and fold over so that it covers the middle third of the dough, then lift up the remaining covered third and fold over the top. Give a quarter (90°) turn, roll out again to a large rectangle, pressing firmly to embed the fruit and lard in the dough, and repeat the scattering and folding action. Give another quarter turn and repeat the rolling, scattering and folding. Now roll out to fit the baking sheet.

5/ Leave to rise in a gently warm but not very warm place for 30–45 minutes. (If too hot, the lard will melt and result in an unpleasantly heavy cake.) While the lardy cake is rising, preheat the oven to 200°C (gas mark 6).

6/ Bake in the preheated oven for 35–40 minutes until brown and well risen. Transfer to a wire rack and leave to cool for a few minutes before turning upside down on the baking sheet so that the melted lard penetrates all the layers. When cool, turn back the right way up and sprinkle generously with caster sugar.
STORAGE: Lardy cake is best eaten very fresh and on the day of making.

Pain d'épices, or spice bread, is a traditional French cake-bread famed for its heady mix of spice and honey. It's made to a very traditional recipe and is particularly, and fondly, associated with Christmas and the pleasures of festive baking. *Pain d'épices* is different to many other European gingerbreads in that it is made with rye flour and only a small amount of sugar, so is dark, firm and quite plain. It slices and toasts well, and is often served with jam for breakfast.

pain d'épices

FOR THE CAKE

400g plain flour
75g rye flour
20g baking powder
½ teaspoon salt
spice: ¼ teaspoon grated nutmeg,
    ¼ teaspoon ground allspice,
    1 teaspoon ginger, a generous pinch
    each of ground cloves and ground
    cardamom OR use up to a total
    of 4 teaspoons of a mixture of
    ground cinnamon, nutmeg, ginger,
    cloves or cardamom according to
    taste and preference
50g soft dark brown sugar
finely grated zest of 1 orange and
    1 lemon (unwaxed or well washed)
300ml clear, runny honey
150ml milk
50g butter, melted, plus extra
    for greasing
1 egg, lightly beaten

YOU WILL NEED

a loaf tin, about 24 x 14 x 7cm,
greased with butter and lined with
baking parchment

makes 1 large loaf
(serves 12–14)

1/ Preheat the oven to 180°C (gas mark 4).
2/ Put the flours, baking powder, salt, spices, sugar, orange and lemon zest into a large mixing bowl. Put the honey, milk, melted butter and egg in a large jug and stir gently to mix.
3/ Make a well in the centre of the dry ingredients and add the liquids. Mix well with a wooden spoon or flexible spatula, until the ingredients are thoroughly and evenly combined. Pour the mixture into the prepared tin and smooth the surface with the back of a large spoon.
4/ Bake in the preheated oven for 60–70 minutes until the loaf is well risen, springy to the touch, cracked along its top, and a metal skewer or sharp knife inserted into the centre of the cake comes out clean. Transfer to a wire rack and leave to cool for 15 minutes before turning out of the tin.
5/ When completely cool, wrap in foil and store in a cool place until you are ready to serve it.
STORAGE: Pain d'épices can be eaten on the day of making, but the flavour and texture develop over the course of 2–4 days.

Treacle has been used in cake-making ever since sugar has been refined on an industrial scale. Its blackness, stickiness and burnt-toffee taste have been used to great effect in dark, dense, spicy cakes that improve with age. Although it's not as popular as it once was, treacle is still a mainstay of the vintage kitchen, and its distinctive taste and unique consistency feature in various treacly treats and cakes that are perfect for cold, winter days.

treacle cake

FOR THE CAKE

120g soft butter, plus extra
    for greasing
120g soft light brown sugar
2 eggs
250g black treacle
3 pieces of candied stem ginger in
    syrup, drained and finely chopped
    (optional)
180g plain flour
1½ teaspoons ground ginger
½ teaspoon bicarbonate of soda
2 tablespoons lukewarm milk

YOU WILL NEED

a 20cm square cake tin, greased with butter and lined with baking parchment

*makes 1 medium cake
(16 squares)*

1/ Preheat the oven to 150°C (gas mark 2).

2/ Put the butter and sugar in a large mixing bowl. With a wooden spoon or an electric whisk, cream them together until they are pale and fluffy. Add the eggs one by one, beating well after each addition.

3/ Measure in the treacle and add the chopped stem ginger (if using). Stir to mix. Sift in the flour and ground ginger.

4/ Mix the bicarbonate of soda with the milk and add to the bowl. Lightly mix all of the ingredients together with a large metal spoon or flexible spatula, to give a thick batter. Spoon the batter into the prepared tin. Level the surface with the back of the spoon or spatula.

5/ Bake in the preheated oven for 1 hour until shiny on the surface and a metal skewer or sharp knife inserted into the centre of the cake comes out clean.

6/ Transfer to a wire rack and leave to cool before turning out of the tin. When cold, wrap in greaseproof paper or aluminium foil and store in an airtight tin. Cut into squares just before serving.

STORAGE: This cake keeps well for 4–5 days and improves with time.

The shape of this cake has been the same since the 16th century, but the spelling has changed, and continues to be a matter of debate depending on where in Europe you are (although the Kugelhopf is still most closely associated with the Alsace region of France). The shape comes from the special fluted ring mould with a central funnel which ensures the cake is evenly cooked. (It is similar to a Bundt tin; a type of tin now widely available in shops). Although some versions are plain and simple, and some are yeast-risen while others rely on baking powder, this recipe includes butter, sugar, eggs and alcohol-soaked raisins, and makes a lightly sweet and subtly enriched cake that can be served with coffee at any time of the day, breakfast included.

kugelhopf

FOR THE CAKE

150g sultanas
2 tablespoons brandy or kirsch
   (optional)
500g strong white flour
1 teaspoon salt
1 x 7g sachet fast-action yeast
grated zest of 1 lemon (unwaxed or
   well washed)
225–250ml milk
125g soft butter, plus extra melted
   butter for greasing
125g caster sugar
2 eggs, lightly beaten
icing sugar, for dusting

YOU WILL NEED

a 23–25cm Bundt or Kugelhopf tin
(round, with a hole in the middle)

makes 1 large cake
(serves 10–12)

1/ In a small bowl, mix the sultanas in the alcohol (if using) and set aside to soak.
2/ Put the flour, salt, yeast and lemon zest in a large mixing bowl and stir to mix. Gently heat the milk to blood temperature.
3/ Put the butter and sugar in a separate bowl. With a wooden spoon or an electric whisk, cream them together until they are pale and fluffy. Add the eggs one by one, beating well after each addition. Pour in 225ml of the lukewarm milk, add the soaked sultanas and stir to mix.
4/ Add the liquid mix to the dry flour and yeast mix. With a flexible spatula or wooden spoon, mix well for a minute. The dough will come together and will be very sticky. If it seems too dry, add a little more milk. Mix well until all the ingredients are combined. Cover with clingfilm or a damp tea towel and leave in a warm, draught-free place to rise for 2 hours or until it has doubled in size.
5/ Grease the cake tin by brushing it with melted butter.
6/ Knock back the dough and knead for a minute. Transfer to the greased baking tin, pressing the dough in evenly and levelling the surface. Cover again with clingfilm or a damp cloth and leave to rise for an hour. Preheat the oven to 180°C (gas mark 4).
7/ Bake in the preheated oven for 45–50 minutes until well risen and golden brown. Transfer to a wire rack and leave to cool for 10 minutes before carefully turning out of the tin. When cool, dust with icing sugar.
STORAGE: Kugelhopf is at its best on the day of making and does not keep well. It is delicious on its own or sliced and spread with butter.

It's not surprising that pancakes feature in culinary histories all over the world, as they are the ultimate in simple, homely cooking, requiring nothing more than a bowl to mix in and a pan or griddle to cook with. Many European pancakes don't contain a raising agent which means they are thin and flat, but the American version of the pancake is a firm, fluffy, slightly sweet, light-as-air disc that uses baking powder to achieve its depth and texture. It's also very absorbent, which is why it works so well with maple syrup (and plenty of fresh fruit). The mix should be made immediately before cooking, and the pancakes eaten immediately after.

pancakes

FOR THE PANCAKES

75g butter, plus extra for greasing
250ml milk
2 eggs
170g plain flour
4 teaspoons baking powder
   (about 10g)
1/2 teaspoon salt
20g caster sugar
maple syrup, to serve

YOU WILL NEED

a griddle or heavy frying pan

makes 20–24 small pancakes

1/ Put the butter and milk in a small saucepan and gently heat until the butter has melted. Remove from the heat and set aside to cool. Whisk the eggs in small bowl. Sift the flour, baking powder and salt into a large mixing bowl. Add the caster sugar and stir to mix.

2/ When the milk and butter mix has cooled and is just warm, pour over the eggs and whisk well to mix.

3/ Heat up the griddle or pan. When hot, wipe a tiny bit of butter over the surface using a little piece of kitchen paper to do so. It will not need greasing again.

4/ Once you are ready to start cooking the pancakes, make a well in the middle of the dry ingredients and pour in the liquid. With a large wooden spoon, mix lightly until all the ingredients are just combined, but do not overmix.

5/ To make the pancakes, drop spoonfuls of batter onto the hot griddle (use a tablespoon or large metal spoon depending on the size of the pancakes you wish to make). Cook until bubbles break on the surface of the pancake, then flip over and cook the other side until both sides are lightly browned and firm to the touch. Serve immediately drizzled with maple syrup. You could also serve with fresh fruit, such as raspberies, strawberries, blueberries or peaches if like.

STORAGE: Pancakes should be eaten while hot and fresh.

Lemon drizzle cake has won a place in our hearts for its very modern mix of sweetness cut by tart lemony acidity. It's also remarkably popular because of its ease of making, portability, keeping qualities, and because it appears at cake sales everywhere. Previous generations of bakers would have called it lemon syrup cake (or loaf), but the principles are the same. It is a simple sponge raised to a new level by pouring or, in modern parlance, 'drizzling' syrup or icing over the still-warm cake. Some lemon drizzle cakes are sugary and crunchy on top, and others are soft and sticky. This recipe falls into the second category as it is closer to the vintage syrup cakes of yesteryear.

lemon drizzle cake

FOR THE CAKE
175g soft butter, plus extra
    for greasing
175g caster sugar
3 eggs
175g self-raising flour
finely grated zest of 2 lemons
    (unwaxed or well washed)
juice of ½ a lemon

FOR THE SYRUP
100g caster sugar
juice of 2 lemons

YOU WILL NEED
a 20cm round cake tin, greased
with butter and base lined with
baking parchment

*makes 1 medium–large cake
(serves 8–10)*

1/ Preheat the oven to 180°C (gas mark 4).
2/ Put the butter and sugar in a large mixing bowl. With a wooden spoon or an electric whisk, cream them together until they are pale and fluffy.
3/ Add the eggs one by one, beating well after each addition.
4/ Sift in the flour and add the lemon zest and juice. With a large metal spoon, fold in gently but thoroughly until the ingredients are fully combined. Spoon into the prepared tin and level the surface with the back of the spoon.
5/ Bake in the preheated oven for 25–30 minutes until well risen and golden brown, and a metal skewer inserted into the centre of the cake comes out clean.
6/ Meanwhile, towards the end of the baking time, make the syrup. Put the sugar and lemon juice in a small saucepan and heat gently without stirring until the sugar has dissolved. Simmer over a medium heat (again without stirring) until the mixture becomes syrupy (the longer you heat it, the thicker it becomes, but runny syrup will cover the cake better). Remove from the heat and set aside.
7/ Transfer the cake to a wire rack. While the cake is still hot and in the tin, pierce about 12–15 small holes in the cake with a metal skewer or clean knitting needle. Briefly reheat the syrup if it has cooled, and pour evenly over the surface of the cake (still in the tin). Leave to cool completely before removing from the tin.
STORAGE: Lemon drizzle cake will keep for a couple of days if wrapped in greaseproof paper and aluminium foil and stored in an airtight tin in a cool place.

The image of malt loaf benefits from its associations with malt extract, a common dietary supplement after the Second World War. This soft, chewy, slightly sagging and ever-popular cake-bread is held in great affection by families and cyclists, who still slice it and butter it, wrap it up and take it to school, work, and on bike rides. Malt loaf has been made commercially since 1890 and many people still think of it as a shop cake, but a homemade version is infinitely better – and gratifyingly larger.

malt loaf

FOR THE LOAF

130g malt extract (or 2 generous tablespoons)

50g golden syrup (or 1 generous dessertspoon)

50g treacle (or 1 generous dessertspoon)

75ml milk

50g butter, plus extra for greasing

250g mixed dried fruit (e.g. 130g chopped dates, 60g sultanas and 60g raisins)

150g self-raising flour

100g plain flour

½ teaspoon bicarbonate of soda

a pinch of salt

1 egg, lightly beaten

FOR THE GLAZE (OPTIONAL)

1 tablespoon caster sugar

2 tablespoons water

YOU WILL NEED

a loaf tin, about 23 x 14 x 7cm, greased with butter and base lined with baking parchment

makes 1 large loaf
(serves 8–12)

1/ Preheat the oven to 160°C (gas mark 3).

2/ Put the malt extract, golden syrup, treacle, milk and butter into a large saucepan. Warm gently over a low heat until the butter has melted and all of the ingredients are combined, stirring regularly. Add the dried fruits. Set aside to cool.

3/ Measure the flours, bicarbonate of soda and salt into a medium bowl, and stir gently with a spoon or hand to mix.

4/ When the ingredients in the pan have cooled, add the beaten egg and mix well with a spoon.

5/ Sift the flour, bicarbonate of soda and salt into the pan. Mix firmly and thoroughly with a wooden spoon or flexible spatula until combined. Spoon the mixture into the loaf tin and level the surface with the back of the spoon.

6/ Bake in the preheated oven for 55–60 minutes. The malt loaf is ready when it is well risen and firm to the touch, and when a metal skewer or sharp knife inserted into the centre comes out clean. Transfer to a wire rack.

7/ As soon as the cake is out of the oven, make the glaze (if using). Put the sugar and water in a small saucepan and bring to the boil. Do not stir at any point. Simmer gently until it thickens and becomes a runny syrup. Brush the glaze over the surface of the hot loaf, and leave the loaf to cool before turning out of the tin. Serve in slices with butter.

STORAGE: Malt loaf will keep well for 3–5 days wrapped in greaseproof paper in an airtight tin, and many argue that it improves with keeping.

The trick with cheesecake is to use really good, simple ingredients. The best cheesecake cheese of all is curd cheese, which is the one all bakers used to use until it was superseded by cream cheese and ricotta, neither of which are technically cheeses. Traditionally, curd cheesecake had just a thin pastry layer or no base at all, but this recipe takes the best of two worlds. It combines the popular 1970s-style crushed-biscuit base with the traditional, dense, creamy curd-cheese filling, and creates a modern version of a true classic. There is no real substitute for curd cheese, but it you can't find it, use plain full-fat cream cheese (but not the expensive salted cream cheese) instead.

curd cheesecake

FOR THE CHEESECAKE

50g butter, melted, plus extra
  for greasing
200g digestive biscuits
700g curd cheese
  (e.g. three 227g tubs)
2 generous tablespoons soured or
  extra-thick double cream
3 eggs
2 teaspoons vanilla extract
200g caster sugar
2 level tablespoons
  plain flour

YOU WILL NEED

a 20cm round deep
cake tin, greased with
butter and lined with
baking parchment

*makes 1 cheesecake
(serves 10–12)*

1/ Preheat the oven to 150°C (gas mark 2).

2/ First make the biscuit base. In a pan, melt the butter. Crush the biscuits: the best method is to put them in a sealable plastic food bag and bash the biscuits with a rolling pin or your feet, taking care not to let the bag split.

3/ Put the crumbs into the pan and mix well with the butter. Tip into the prepared tin and press down evenly on the base using the palm of your hand (a potato masher also works very well and gives a much more even surface). Bake in the preheated oven for 10 minutes to set. Set aside to cool while you make the filling.

4/ Put the curd cheese, soured or double cream, eggs, vanilla and sugar in a large mixing bowl, and beat well with a whisk or electric mixer until smooth and fully combined. Sift in the flour and mix again until nicely thick and creamy. Pour the mix into the tin and tap a few times to release air bubbles and to obtain a smooth surface.

5/ Bake for 1¼ hours or until the cheesecake has risen and is turning pale gold at the outside edge, but still has a hint of a wobble.

6/ Transfer to a wire rack and leave to cool completely before removing from the tin.

STORAGE: Although it is ready to eat when cool, curd cheesecake improves immeasurably after a night in the fridge, and it will then keep well for 2–3 days. Serve on its own, or with thick pouring cream. Fresh or poached fruits are also delicious with cheesecake.

Little treats that can be wrapped in greaseproof paper and stashed in lunchboxes, school satchels, bicycle baskets and picnic hampers have some of the most evocative names of all. It's difficult not to wax nostalgic at the mention of lamingtons and fat rascals, rock buns and Eccles cakes, and then wonder whatever happened to these cakes that seem to be from a different era of school tuck boxes, cosy tea-rooms and wonderful children's stories. Happily, they have not yet disappeared, and they still offer some of the most enduring and portable tastes of vintage baking, and often come with a delightful story attached to their making. Some are still closely affiliated with their place of origin, some have become world famous. No matter where you are, they are a small, welcome taste of a home kitchen. They are ideal for sheds and dens, any kind of sports match tea, country picnics, cake stalls and community gatherings, and require no more than a hearty appetite to do them justice.

little
cakes

Baron Lamington was the Governor of Queensland, Australia, from 1896–1901 and although we know that these little cakes were named after him, it's not quite clear who came up with the idea of dipping sponge cubes in chocolate and rolling them in desiccated coconut to make a sweet treat that is now part of any antipodean childhood. They are widely available in shops and supermarkets in Australia and New Zealand but, as with all vintage cakes, homemade versions taste better. They are easy to make and children, of course, will love the messiness of helping to dip and roll, and will join the many generations of cake-eaters who look upon Lamingtons with great fondness and nostalgia.

lamingtons

FOR THE CAKES

125g soft butter, plus extra
   for greasing
150g caster sugar
2 eggs
230g plain flour
2 teaspoons baking powder
a generous pinch of salt
1 teaspoon vanilla extract
100ml milk
200g desiccated coconut, to decorate

FOR THE ICING

400g icing sugar
3–4 tablespoons cocoa powder
25g butter
100ml milk

YOU WILL NEED

a 20cm nonstick square cake tin, greased with butter and base lined with baking parchment

makes 16 lamingtons

1/ Preheat the oven to 180°C (gas mark 4).

2/ Put the butter and sugar in a large mixing bowl. With a wooden spoon or an electric whisk, cream them together until they are pale and fluffy. Add the eggs one by one, beating well after each addition.

3/ Sift together the flour, baking powder and salt into a small bowl. Mix the vanilla extract with the milk in a measuring jug. Add half the flour mixture to the ingredients in the large mixing bowl, followed by half the milk and vanilla. With a large metal spoon or flexible spatula, fold in gently. Add the rest of the flour and milk, and continue folding in gently until thoroughly combined.

4/ Spoon the mixture into the prepared tin and level the surface with the back of the spoon or spatula. Bake in the preheated oven for 30 minutes until well risen and springy to the touch, and a metal skewer inserted into the centre of the sponge comes out clean. Transfer to a wire rack. Leave to cool before turning out of the tin.

5/ When the cake has cooled completely and you are ready to ice it, cut the sponge into 16 squares (or 25 smaller squares if preferred).

6/ To make the icing, sift the icing sugar and cocoa powder into a large mixing bowl. Add the butter and milk and mix well to create a smooth, slightly runny icing that will cover the sponge squares without running off.

7/ Put the desiccated coconut into a wide bowl or onto a large plate. Using your hands or a fork, first dip the squares into the icing OR spread with a knife, covering all sides except the base. Then quickly roll the squares in the desiccated coconut until evenly coated. Transfer to a wire rack to dry. Continue until all the squares have been iced and dipped in coconut.

STORAGE: Lamingtons are best stored in an airtight tin in a cool place and eaten within a day or two of making.

Rock buns or cakes have often unjustly been the butt of many baking jokes. Too often hard, dry and rocky by nature as well as by name, they have come to epitomise a mean, austere style of vintage baking. Yet when they are made with plenty of butter, soft brown sugar, a generous helping of plump dried fruit, a waft of nutmeg and a grating of lemon zest, they can be utterly, meltingly delicious. Rock buns need to be large and filling, the kind of thing you'd be happy to find in a cake tin after a long walk or an energetic game, or for a rather good elevenses on any day of the week.

rock buns

FOR THE BUNS

340g plain flour
2 teaspoons baking powder
½ teaspoon salt
a good grating of fresh nutmeg
a pinch of mixed spice (optional)
170g light soft brown sugar
100–150g undyed glacé cherries
100g raisins
70g sultanas OR
    a total of 250–300g mixed dried
    fruit, according to taste and what's
    in the cupboard
finely grated zest of 1 lemon (unwaxed
    or well washed)
170g butter at room temperature,
    but not too soft
1 large egg
1–2 tablespoons milk

YOU WILL NEED

1 large baking sheet, lined with baking
parchment

makes 12 buns

1/ Preheat the oven to 180°C (gas mark 4).
2/ Sift the flour, baking powder, salt, nutmeg and spice (if using) into a large bowl. Add the sugar and stir a couple of times with your hand or a spoon to mix.
3/ Prepare the dried fruit. Rinse the cherries to remove any excess syrup, and pat dry with a kitchen towel. Slice each cherry in half and put them in a separate large bowl with the raisins and sultanas (or whatever dried fruit you are using). Add the finely grated lemon zest and stir with your hand or a spoon to mix.
4/ Add the butter to the flour mix and use your fingertips to rub the dry ingredients and butter together until the mix resembles fine sandy breadcrumbs. Make sure there are no lumps of butter remaining. Stir in the dried fruit and lemon zest.
5/ Crack the egg into a small bowl or cup, add a tablespoon of milk, and whisk well with a fork until combined.
6/ Make a well in the centre of the dry mixture and add the egg and milk. With the fork, mix quickly and lightly until the ingredients come together in a stiff-ish, firm, slightly sticky dough. The mixture should do this quite easily without too much pressure. Do not overwork. If it is still on the dry and crumbly side, add a little more milk very sparingly. Be careful not to make the mixture too slack or it will turn into flat cookies when in the oven.
7/ Using your hands or 2 forks, pile the mixture into 12 individual 'rocks' (craggy piles) on the prepared baking sheet. Bake in the preheated oven for 17–20 minutes until the buns are golden brown, with the tiniest hint of squishiness on top. They will continue to cook when you have taken them out of the oven. Transfer to a wire rack and leave the buns to cool (although they are quite delicious when still warm – not hot – with a glass of milk or a cup of tea).
STORAGE: Rock buns are delicious when fresh, but also keep well for up to 2 days if stored in an airtight tin in a cool place.

Devonshire splits are the local county name for jammy buns, the treats beloved by many a children's book character and generations of more mature takers of cream teas. They are a classic: soft balls of rich, sweet dough that are then split diagonally and filled to bursting with jam and cream. Although they have been overlooked in recent times in favour of the quicker scone, these buns are very easy to make and are ideal for a large, hungry party.

devonshire splits

FOR THE BUNS

1 x 7g sachet fast-action dried yeast
1 teaspoon clear runny honey or
    caster sugar
450ml milk
680g strong white flour, plus extra
    for dusting
15g salt
120g butter

TO FINISH & FILL

icing sugar, for dusting
jam
whipped cream

YOU WILL NEED

1 or 2 baking sheets, lined with
baking parchment

makes 16–20 buns
(depending on size)

1/ Put the yeast and honey or sugar in a bowl. Gently heat the milk in a saucepan to blood temperature (lukewarm, no hotter), then pour over the yeast and honey in the bowl. Stir to mix, and set aside.

2/ Put the flour, salt and butter in a mixing bowl. Rub in the butter using your fingertips, until the mixture resembles fine crumbs. Make a well in the centre and pour in the liquid ingredients. With your hand, mix to a soft, slightly sticky dough.

3/ Turn out onto a floured work surface (don't wash the bowl). Knead for 5 minutes until the dough is smooth and elastic. Shape into a squat ball. Lightly oil the mixing bowl and return the dough to the bowl. Cover with clingfilm or a damp cloth and leave in a warm place to rise until it has doubled in size. This will take 1½–2½ hours depending on the temperature of the room.

4/ Punch down the dough – with a floured hand, press down the dough to knock out the air. Turn out of the bowl onto a floured work surface. Knead lightly for 1 minute. Divide the dough into 16–20 equal pieces, depending on how many splits you want to make. Electronic scales will help you to be accurate. Roll each piece into a smooth ball and place in rows well apart on the baking sheet(s). Cover with oiled clingfilm and leave to rise for 20–30 minutes. While the dough is rising, preheat the oven to 200°C (gas mark 6).

5/ Bake for 20 minutes or until the buns are well risen, golden brown, and sound hollow when tapped on the base. Put the baking sheet on a wire rack, and remove the buns from the sheet after a couple of minutes. Dust with icing sugar while still hot. Let the buns cool. When you are ready to serve, make a diagonal cut through each bun (without slicing completely). Fill with a layer of jam then a layer of whipped cream, and eat straightaway.
STORAGE: Eat Devonshire splits on the day of making.

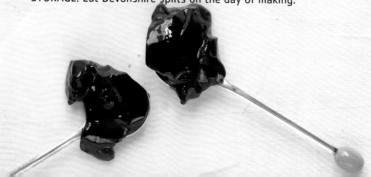

It's no wonder chocolate brownies have been adopted so enthusiastically by cake-lovers beyond their native America; the combination of rich chocolate flavour and chewy, fudgy texture is irresistible. They are supremely easy to make, and can be eaten on their own as an indulgent snack or with cream as a pudding. They are very portable and make a delicious picnic or party treat and, should it ever happen that they are not all eaten immediately, they keep well for several days. For best results, use good-quality dark chocolate, and take care with the baking time as a slightly undercooked brownie is the best sort.

brownies

FOR THE BROWNIES

300g dark chocolate (70% cocoa solids)
120g plain flour
20g good-quality cocoa powder
½ teaspoon baking powder
½–¾ teaspoon salt
4 eggs, lightly whisked with a fork
250g soft butter, plus extra for greasing
300g golden caster sugar
icing sugar, to decorate (optional)

YOU WILL NEED

a 23cm square baking tin, greased with butter and lined with baking parchment or greaseproof paper

makes 12–16 brownies

1/ Preheat the oven to 180°C (gas mark 4).

2/ Break the chocolate into squares and melt in a bowl suspended over a saucepan of just-boiled water, with the water level coming halfway up the bowl. Take care not to get any water in the chocolate. Leave for 5 minutes to melt, stirring once or twice. When the chocolate is fully melted, remove the bowl from the pan and set aside to cool a little.

3/ Sift the flour, cocoa powder, baking powder and salt into a bowl. Crack the eggs into a separate bowl and whisk lightly with a fork.

4/ Put the butter and sugar in a large mixing bowl. With a wooden spoon or an electric whisk, cream them together until they are pale and fluffy. Gradually add the beaten eggs, beating well after each addition.

5/ Now add the melted chocolate, the sifted flour, baking powder and salt and fold in gently and thoroughly with a flexible spatula or large metal spoon, making sure there are no pale streaks. Do not rush this; be patient and fold in until the mixture looks (and tastes) like a rich chocolate mousse.

6/ Spoon the mix into the prepared tin and smooth the surface. Bake in the preheated oven for 25–30 minutes. The top will rise and have a slightly crackled, bubbly surface and the centre will still have a hint of a wobble. When done, a skewer or sharp knife should come out with some sticky brownie on it, but not uncooked mixture. Check after 25 minutes and, if necessary, leave in the oven for a further 2–3 minutes, but do not walk away and forget the brownies as they can overcook in no time at all. The point of brownies is that they come out of the oven looking slightly undercooked and sticky – they should not be dry and spongy.

7/ When done, leave the brownies to cool completely in their tin on a wire rack before slicing into squares. If you try to cut them when warm, it makes the edges very messy. If desired, sift a little icing sugar over the brownies to finish.

STORAGE: Brownies keep well for 2–3 days stored in an airtight tin in a cool place.

These charmingly named, scone-like cakes are a speciality of Yorkshire and north-east England, where they have been baked since Elizabethan times. Originally made from scraps of dough cooked over turf fires, they are now associated with the more genteel surroundings of Bettys Tea Rooms in York and other nearby towns in Yorkshire. They are still as large as ever, though, and should be eaten fresh, warm, split and buttered.

fat rascals

FOR THE CAKES

275g self-raising flour
a pinch of salt
a grating of nutmeg or pinch of mixed
    spice (optional)
100g cold butter, cubed
100g caster sugar
150g mixed dried fruit (ready mixed
    or your own choice of fruit, such
    as sultanas, raisins, currants or
    candied peel)
150ml double cream plus 1 teaspoon
    lemon juice (or use soured cream)
1 egg, lightly beaten

TO DECORATE

2 or 3 whole blanched almonds and a
glacé cherry sliced in half per fat rascal

YOU WILL NEED

1 baking sheet, lined with baking
parchment.

makes 8 fat rascals

1/ Preheat the oven to 200°C (gas mark 6).

2/ Sift the flour, salt and spice (if using) into a large mixing bowl.

3/ Add the butter and rub it into the dry ingredients using your fingertips, until the mixture looks like fine breadcrumbs. Add the sugar and fruit and stir to mix.

4/ Measure out the cream in a jug and add the lemon juice (if using). Stir the cream – it will thicken and stiffen as you go, but take care not to overmix. Alternatively, measure out the soured cream in the jug.

5/ Add this to the bowl along with the beaten egg. Stir with a wooden spoon or flexible spatula to make a soft, sticky dough. With floured hands, make 8 balls and place well apart on the baking sheet. Decorate each with 2–3 blanched almonds and a glacé cherry sliced in half.

6/ Bake in the preheated oven for 22–25 minutes until the fat rascals have expanded, risen, and are golden brown.

7/ Transfer to a wire rack, and leave to cool, taking the cakes off the sheet after 5 minutes. Serve fresh and warm, whole or split and spread with butter, preferably on the day of making.

STORAGE: Fat rascals are at their best on the day of making, although they make a pleasant and welcome elevenses treat the following day. Store in an airtight tin in a cool place.

almond slices

chelsea buns

'Slices' have always had an air of bakery poshness, even though they are one of the most widely available baked treats of all. This one is the first cousin of the Bakewell tart, but without any claims to historical accuracy. With their buttery mix of pastry, sponge, jam and nut topping, homemade slices beat shop-bought slices hands down.

almond slices

FOR THE BASE
200g plain flour
50g ground almonds
50g caster sugar
125g soft butter, plus extra
   for greasing
1 egg, lightly beaten

FOR THE TOPPING & FILLING
125g soft butter
125g caster sugar
2 eggs
125g ground almonds
75g self-raising flour
4–6 tablespoons raspberry jam
   (about 300g)
a handful of flaked almonds

YOU WILL NEED
a Swiss roll tin, about 20 x 30cm,
greased with butter

makes 16–20 slices

1/ Begin by making the shortbread base which needs to be chilled before baking. Put the flour, almonds and sugar into a bowl. Add the butter and rub it in with your fingertips until the mixture resembles large breadcrumbs. Add the egg. With a knife or your hand, mix well to bring the ingredients together into a soft, sticky dough.
2/ Press the dough out in the tin so that it is evenly distributed, making sure you push the dough into the corners and out to the edges. Prick the dough all over with a fork (about 12–16 times), cover with clingfilm and chill in the fridge for at least 1 hour. Before you take the tin out of the fridge, preheat the oven to 180°C (gas mark 4).
3/ Bake the shortbread base in the preheated oven for 15–20 minutes until the biscuit base is dry and just beginning to change colour, but do not overcook. Transfer to a wire rack and leave to cool for 10–15 minutes. Leave the oven on if you are continuing with the recipe. If not, turn off and remember to preheat again to 180°C (gas mark 4) when you are ready to make the topping.
4/ While the base is cooling, make the frangipane topping. Put the butter and sugar in a large mixing bowl. With a wooden spoon or an electric whisk, cream them together until they are pale and fluffy. Add the eggs one by one, beating well after each addition. Add the ground almonds and flour. With a large metal spoon, fold in gently until the ingredients are thoroughly and evenly mixed.
5/ Spread a layer of raspberry jam over the shortbread base. Then spread the frangipane mix to cover the jam. You need to do this very gently and carefully to avoid mixing the sponge mix with the jam. The mix will spread a little during baking, so if it is uneven around the edges, it doesn't matter too much. Sprinkle with flaked almonds.
6/ Bake for 22–25 minutes until risen and golden brown. Test with a metal skewer or sharp knife: if it comes outs clean the almond slice is done. Transfer to a wire rack and leave to cool completely before removing from the tin. To remove, cut into 16–20 slices with a sharp knife or bread knife. Carefully lift out a slice with a palette knife. Once one slice has been removed, it's easy to lift out the rest.
STORAGE: Almond slices will keep well for up to 3 days if wrapped in foil and stored in an airtight tin in a cool place.

Sadly, the famous Chelsea Bun House closed in 1839 after a few glorious decades of selling its buns to ordinary Londoners and royalty alike. But the recipe survived and the distinctive spiral in the squashed square shape is still instantly recognisable. Although a good Chelsea bun is a generous mix of sweetened dough, sugar, butter and fruit, it's never overpowering, heavy or sweet, which is no doubt why 18th-century Londoners flocked to buy them.

chelsea buns

FOR THE BUNS

1 x 7g sachet fast-action dried yeast or 1 level dessertspoon dried yeast
1 teaspoon sugar
250ml milk
500g strong plain flour, plus extra for dusting
1 teaspoon salt
50g cold butter, cubed
50g caster sugar, plus extra for sprinkling (optional)
1 egg

FOR THE FILLING

50g butter, melted
75g dark soft brown sugar or dark muscovado sugar
150g mixed dried fruit (raisins, sultanas, currants)

FOR THE GLAZE

2–3 tablespoons milk
1–2 tablespoon caster sugar

YOU WILL NEED

1 baking sheet, lined with baking parchment

makes 16 buns

1/ Make the yeast starter first following the instructions on page 17. Put the remaining 400g flour and the salt in a large mixing bowl. Add the butter and rub into the flour with your fingertips until it resembles very fine sandy breadcrumbs. Add the sugar and stir to mix.

2/ Pour the yeast mix onto the flour, add the egg, and with your hand, bring the ingredients together into a soft, rough dough. Turn out onto a floured work surface and knead for 4–5 minutes until the dough is smooth and pliable, and starts to feel slightly clammy. Form into a ball. Lightly oil the mixing bowl (no need to wash before doing this) and return the dough to the bowl. Roll the ball round the bowl to ensure it picks up a very light coating of oil. Cover the bowl with clingfilm and leave to rise in a warm, draught-free place for 1½–2 hours until doubled in size (the time taken depends on the room temperature).

3/ With floured hands, punch down the dough and turn it onto a lightly floured work surface. Knead for a minute until all the air has been knocked out. Divide the dough into two equal pieces. Roll out each one into a rectangle about 35 x 20cm. Brush with melted butter, sprinkle with brown sugar, then scatter the dried fruit on top.

4/ Starting at the wider end, roll up into a tight roll, pressing firmly as you roll. Pinch the seam together tightly (a little milk brushed over helps) to prevent the roll undoing. Trim the ends, and cut each roll into 8 pieces, each about 3cm long.

5/ Place on the baking sheet, cut side up and almost touching (about 1–2cm apart). The buns will expand and touch during rising and baking. Cover with a piece of lightly oiled clingfilm and leave in a warm place to rise for 45 minutes. Towards the end of the rising period, preheat the oven to 200°C (gas mark 6).

6/ Put the buns in the preheated oven and bake for 20 minutes before brushing with the glaze, which should be made just before you need it. To do this, heat the milk in a saucepan until it is very hot but not boiling, take off the heat, add the sugar and mix well with the brush you are using. Open the oven, pull out the sheet halfway, and brush the buns with the glaze. Return to the oven and bake for a further 5 minutes until the buns are brown and shiny.

7/ Remove from the oven and transfer to a wire rack. Sprinkle with sugar (if using) and leave to cool. Pull the buns apart when you are ready to serve them.

STORAGE: Chelsea buns are at their best on the day of making and lose their freshness very quickly. They are delicious on their own.

Recipe leaflets produced in the 1930s and 1940s by major flour companies can often be found in secondhand bookshops, and frequently contain little gems. The recipes are frill-free, and are very plain by comparison with today's recipes, as they focus on cheap and available ingredients such as flour and jam. Raspberry jam cakes are a fine example of this plain-but-good vintage baking, but using high-quality jam and butter will elevate them to a new taste level.

raspberry jam cakes

FOR THE CAKES

250g self-raising flour, plus extra for dusting

1 teaspoon baking powder

85g cold butter, cubed

85g caster sugar, plus extra for sprinkling

1 large egg, beaten

2–3 tablespoons milk, plus extra for brushing

about 6 teaspoons raspberry jam (don't use soft-set or very runny jam as this will make closing up the cakes messy and difficult)

YOU WILL NEED

1 baking sheet, lined with baking parchment

makes 12 cakes

1/ Preheat the oven to 180°C (gas mark 4).

2/ Sift the flour and baking powder into a large bowl. Add the butter and rub it into the flour with your fingertips, until it resembles fine sandy breadcrumbs. Add the sugar and stir to distribute evenly.

3/ With a fork, mix the egg with a tablespoon of milk first and then add it to the contents of the bowl. With a round-ended knife or your hands, bring the ingredients together to make a soft, damp, but not sticky dough. Add a little more milk if necessary (it is unlikely you will need more than 2–3 tablespoons of milk).

4/ On a lightly floured surface, using your hands and working quickly, shape the dough into a flattish rectangle and divide into 12 roughly equal pieces with a knife. Roll each piece into a ball.

5/ Flatten each ball slightly, then make a little depression in the centre and bring the edges up, as if you were making a very basic clay pot. Place half a teaspoon of raspberry jam in the middle of each cake.

6/ With your fingers, gently bring the edges together to close the dough over the jam. Then turn the cakes over and place them well apart on the prepared baking sheet. Brush the tops with milk and sprinkle each cake with a little caster sugar.

7/ Bake in the preheated oven for 15–20 minutes until the cakes are pale gold, but not brown. Do not overcook them, as you want to keep them relatively moist. If you cook them too long they become biscuity.

8/ Transfer to a wire rack and leave the cakes to cool before eating. Do not eat straight from the oven as the hot jam could burn. Pile them on a plate and serve with tea.

STORAGE: Raspberry jam cakes are at their best on the day of making.

Eccles cakes have been made in the Lancashire town of that name since 1793, and have changed very little since. The basics of buttery flaky or puff pastry, a dense, curranty filling, a whiff of spice and a topping of caster sugar are so simple they endure as the perfect pastry package of sweetness and texture. They are delicious, eat-anywhere cakes with a proud history, and can be made quickly and easily.

eccles cakes

FOR THE CAKES

50g butter
100g dark soft brown sugar
250g currants
a good grating of nutmeg
500g puff pastry (such as ready-rolled all-butter puff pastry)
1 egg white, lightly beaten
caster sugar, for sprinkling

YOU WILL NEED

1 or 2 baking sheets, lined with baking parchment
a 7–9cm round cutter

makes 12–16 cakes

1/ Preheat the oven to 220°C (gas mark 7).

2/ Make the filling first. Put the butter and sugar into a saucepan and melt gently, stirring to mix. Take off the heat, add the currants and nutmeg. Mix well; set aside.

3/ Roll out the puff pastry (if not using ready-rolled) to a thickness of about 4–5mm. Using the cutter, cut out as many circles as you can from the pastry, making sure you have an equal number. Place half the circles on the baking sheet(s), spaced well apart.

4/ Spoon a heap of the currant filling onto each of the circles on the sheet(s). Top with a second circle of pastry and press and pinch the outer edge to seal. Brush with beaten egg white and sprinkle generously with caster sugar. Make 2 or 3 cuts in the top of each Eccles cake with a sharp knife or pair of scissors.

5/ Bake in the preheated oven for 12–15 minutes until puffed up and the tops are a deep, caramelised golden-brown, taking care not to let them burn. Serve warm or cold, but do not eat straight from the oven as the filling will be blisteringly hot.

STORAGE: Eccles cakes are at their best on the day of making, but will keep well for a day or two if stored in an airtight tin in a cool place.

These little almondy cakes originated in France where they are better known as 'financiers', a name derived from the traditional long, rectangular shape that resembles a bar of gold, and from the cakes' historical link with the financial district of Paris. These days you are more likely to find them labelled 'friands' and made in a distinctive oval shape. They are extremely *à la mode* in Australia and, unsurprisingly, their popularity is spreading.

friands

FOR THE FRIANDS

175g butter, plus extra for greasing
200g icing sugar
60g flour
120g ground almonds
a pinch of salt
finely grated zest of 1 lemon (unwaxed and well washed)
5 egg whites
1 or 2 raspberries per friand

YOU WILL NEED

an 8-hole silicone friand mould, brushed with melted butter, placed on a baking sheet for ease of carrying. Alternatively, use a muffin tin and grease well with butter

makes 16–18 friands

1/ Preheat the oven to 200°C (gas mark 6).

2/ Put the butter in a small saucepan and heat gently to melt. Allow to simmer and sizzle for several minutes until the liquid has turned golden brown and smells nutty. Take care not to burn the butter. Set aside to cool.

3/ Sift the icing sugar and flour into a medium bowl, preferably one with a lip (see cook's tip below). Add the ground almonds, salt and lemon zest and stir to mix.

4/ Put the egg whites in a small bowl and whisk with a fork until they break up and start to foam on the surface. Add to the dry ingredients and mix well with a wooden spoon or flexible spatula. Pour in the melted butter and mix until fully combined. If you are not using a bowl with a lip, pour the mix into a large jug.

5/ Pour the mix into the prepared moulds, filling each one half full. Top each one with 1 or 2 raspberries. Bake in the preheated oven for 15–20 minutes until golden brown and well risen. Transfer to a wire rack and leave to cool before gently turning out of the moulds. Repeat until all the mixture has been used.

STORAGE: Friands are delicious when absolutely fresh, although they are still almost as good the day after if stored in an airtight tin.

cook's tips

For this recipe, a mixing bowl with a lip is ideal as it helps with pouring the mix into the mould later on. If not, transfer the mix to a jug when it is ready to be poured.

Adjust the baking time if making larger or smaller friands, depending on the size of your mould or tin.

Poppy seeds are a feature of Central and Eastern European baking where you can find a vast array of darkly speckled cakes and breads that use the seeds as a filling or a topping. This recipe marries the poppy seed with another European baking tradition, that of the circular Bundt cake which is baked in a special tin with a central tube. Both traditions have been adopted enthusiastically elsewhere, and since the 1960s there has been a proliferation of fabulously shaped tins, especially in the US. This recipe can be used to make mini Bundt cakes in moulded shapes (or in plain muffin cases), or one large, gracefully shaped cake.

poppy seed bundt cakes

FOR THE CAKES
30g poppy seeds
200ml milk
225g soft butter
225g caster sugar
3 eggs
325g plain flour
2 heaped teaspoons baking powder

YOU WILL NEED
2 mini Bundt trays or 1 large 20cm Bundt tin, brushed with melted butter OR two 12-hole muffin trays lined with paper muffin cases

makes 20–24 mini Bundt cakes or muffins or 1 large Bundt cake (serves 10–12)

1/ Preheat the oven to 180°C (gas mark 4).

2/ Put the poppy seeds in a small bowl. In a small saucepan, gently heat the milk until almost boiling. Pour over the poppy seeds and set aside.

3/ Put the butter and sugar in a large mixing bowl. With a wooden spoon or an electric whisk, cream them together until they are pale and fluffy. Add the eggs one by one, beating well after each addition.

4/ Sift in half the flour and baking powder, and add half the milk with poppy seeds. With a wooden spoon or flexible spatula, fold in gently. Add the rest of the ingredients and continue folding in until fully combined and smooth.

5/ Spoon into the prepared tin(s) or cases. If using a large Bundt tin, level the surface with the back of the spoon or spatula. Bake in the preheated oven until well risen, pale golden brown, and a metal skewer or sharp knife inserted into the centre of a cake comes out clean (15–20 minutes for small cakes or muffins and 55–60 minutes for a large Bundt cake).

6/ Transfer to a wire rack and leave to cool for a few minutes before gently turning out of the tin(s). Leave to cool completely.

STORAGE: Poppy seed Bundt cakes are delicious on the day of making, although they will keep for another day if kept in an airtight tin. They also freeze well.

Maids of honour cakes are a dainty taste of Tudor history –
delightful little sweetmeats that were served to Anne Boleyn and
her maids of honour, until Henry VIII appropriated the recipe for
himself, or so the story goes. Today, there is an Original Maids of
Honour tea room in Richmond, near London, that uses a closely
guarded secret recipe, but in fact they are very simple to make at
home, and are a direct line to baking history.

maids of honour

FOR THE CAKES
flour, for dusting
375g pack chilled all-butter puff pastry
225g curd cheese (or a 227g tub)
50g caster sugar
30g ground almonds
1 egg and 1 egg yolk
grated zest of 1 lemon (optional)
2–3 tablespoons lemon curd (see page
    141, optional)

YOU WILL NEED
two 12-hole jam tart tins
a 7–8cm round cutter

makes 18–20 cakes

1/ Preheat the oven to 220°C (gas mark 7).

2/ On a lightly floured work surface, roll out the puff pastry to a thickness of
2–3mm, large enough to cut out 18–20 circles with a 7–8cm cutter. Line the tins
with the pastry circles.

3/ Now make the filling. In a large mixing bowl, put the curd cheese, caster sugar,
ground almonds, egg, egg yolk and lemon zest (if using). Combine with a wooden
spoon or flexible spatula until smooth and evenly mixed.

4/ If using lemon curd, spoon half a teaspoon into each pastry case (but no more
as it expands dramatically during baking). Spoon a dessertspoonful of the curd
mixture into each case.

5/ Bake in the preheated oven in two batches for 20–22 minutes until puffed
up and golden brown on top. Transfer to a wire rack and leave to cool for a few
minutes before lifting them out of the tin. Leave to cool completely, or serve while
still just faintly warm.

STORAGE: Maids of honour do not keep well and should be eaten fresh and on the
day of making.

Recipes for queen cakes date back as far as the 18th century, and are surprisingly consistent. They are all made with honest-to-goodness butter, sugar, flour and eggs, and while currants are obligatory, rose water or orange flower water are optional. They are simple and good, and were of course patriotically popular when Queen Victoria was on the throne. They have always been baked in small, individual tins (or 'patty pans'), sometimes heart-shaped, which is why they are also often called heart cakes. (Now that we have nonstick silicone moulds, it's easy to replicate this.) It's the kind of recipe that children love making: simple and with a delicious mix to lick out of the bowl, plus very pretty results.

queen cakes

FOR THE CAKES
125g soft butter
125g caster sugar
2 eggs
150g plain flour
1 teaspoon baking powder
finely grated zest of 1 lemon (unwaxed
    or well washed)
125g currants
a splash of milk

YOU WILL NEED
a 6 or 8-hole heart-shaped silicone
mould OR a 12-hole bun tin, lined
with paper cases

makes 12 cakes

1/ Preheat the oven to 180°C (gas mark 4).
2/ Put the butter and sugar in a large mixing bowl. With a wooden spoon or an electric whisk, cream them together until they are pale and fluffy. Add the eggs one by one, beating well after each addition.
3/ Sift in the flour and baking powder and add the lemon zest and currants. With a large metal spoon or flexible spatula, mix in gently, adding a splash of milk to give a soft, gently dropping consistency. Spoon the mixture into the heart-shaped cases, filling each one two-thirds full.
4/ Bake in the preheated oven for 20 minutes until well risen and springy to the touch. Transfer to a wire rack and leave to cool for 5–10 minutes before removing the cakes from the mould or tin to cool completely. Repeat if necessary to use up any remaining cake mixture. Serve immediately.

STORAGE: Queen cakes are delicious when fresh, and will keep for a day longer if stored in an airtight tin in a cool place.

As long ago as the late 18th century, cakes were often baked in small, individual cups, giving rise to the name 'cupcake'. In America, the name fell into common use, whereas in Britain it only caught on more recently. Modern cupcakes are larger, deeper, fancier and more colourful than their altogether more dainty British counterparts, fairy cakes (see page 180), and in recent years have wooed cake-eaters everywhere with their good looks and exuberance. Today's cupcakes are a mini-celebration in a single cake, a sweet little gift or a delicious indulgence.

cupcakes

FOR THE CUPCAKES

200g plain flour
1½ teaspoons baking powder
¾ teaspoon salt
4 eggs
350g dark soft brown sugar or dark muscovado sugar
30g butter
2 teaspoons vanilla extract

FOR THE FROSTING

175g dark soft brown sugar or dark muscovado sugar
60ml double cream
50g soft butter
a pinch of salt
175g icing sugar

TO DECORATE (OPTIONAL)

edible glitter (gold looks particularly fetching) or sprinkles of your choice

YOU WILL NEED

a 12-hole muffin tin, lined with paper muffin cases

makes 12 cupcakes

dark brown sugar cupcakes with brown sugar frosting

1/ Preheat the oven to 180°C (gas mark 4).

2/ You will need a good-size mixing bowl set over a saucepan of just-simmering water. Make sure the bowl fits and bring the water to the boil before beginning the preparation.

3/ Sift the flour, baking powder and salt into a small bowl. Off the heat, put the eggs in the mixing bowl and whisk lightly with a fork. Add the sugar and butter and stir to mix. Set the bowl over the pan of water on a gentle heat (take care not to let it boil over). With a wooden spoon or flexible spatula, stir constantly until the mix is very warm.

4/ Remove the bowl from the pan of water, and add the dry ingredients. Mix well, adding the vanilla extract, until smooth and well blended.

5/ Spoon the mix into the muffin cases, dividing it equally and filling each case about half full. Bake in the preheated oven for 20–22 minutes until the cupcakes are well risen and springy to the touch, and a toothpick or fine skewer inserted into the centre comes out clean.

6/ Transfer to a wire rack and leave to cool before removing the cupcakes from the tin. Leave the cupcakes to cool completely before frosting.

7/ To make the frosting: put the sugar, cream, butter and salt in a large saucepan. Bring to the boil slowly over a medium heat, stirring constantly. Then boil gently for 5 minutes without stirring at all. Remove the pan from the heat and leave to cool for 20–30 minutes.

8/ Sift in the icing sugar and with a wooden spoon or flexible spatula, beat well until smooth and spreadable. Add a little more cream if necessary in order to get a consistency that will spread or pipe well.

9/ Working quickly, as this frosting sets quite rapidly, either spread the frosting over the cupcakes with a palette knife, or pipe on using a star-shaped nozzle. Decorate as desired.

STORAGE: These are best eaten fresh as they do not keep well, although these particular cupcakes will keep for a day before or after they have been iced.

FOR THE CUPCAKES

300g plain flour
2½ teaspoons baking powder
a pinch of salt
200g caster sugar
125ml water
2 teaspoons vanilla extract
3 egg whites
275ml double cream

FOR THE FROSTING

250g icing sugar
75g soft butter
20–30ml milk
a few drops of vanilla extract (optional)
sprinkles, silver balls, edible glitter,
   to decorate (optional)

YOU WILL NEED

two 12-hole muffins tins, lined with
16 paper muffin cases

makes 16 cupcakes

whipped cream cupcakes with vanilla frosting

1/ Preheat the oven to 180°C (gas mark 4).

2/ Sift the flour, baking powder and salt into a bowl. Add the caster sugar and stir to mix. Measure out the water in a jug and add the vanilla. In a separate clean bowl, whisk the egg whites until they form soft peaks. In a large mixing bowl, whisk the cream until fluffy and billowing.

3/ With a large metal spoon or flexible spatula, gently fold the egg whites into the cream until fully combined. Now pour in the water/vanilla mix and stir lightly to just combine. Add the dry ingredients a little at a time, folding in gently and thoroughly after each addition until you have a cake batter with no flecks of flour.

4/ Spoon the mixture into the muffin cases, dividing it evenly and filling each case about half full. Bake in the preheated oven for 20–25 minutes until risen and golden brown, and a fine toothpick or metal skewer inserted into the centre of a cupcake comes out clean. Transfer to a wire rack and leave to cool for a few minutes before turning out of the baking tins. Leave to cool completely before covering with frosting.

5/ To make the frosting, sift the icing sugar into a mixing bowl and add the butter. Pour in a little milk and a few drops of vanilla extract (if using), and start beating with a wooden spoon or electric mixer. Gradually add more milk until you have a smooth, spreadable mix. Continue beating vigorously for 2–3 minutes until pale, light and fluffy; the longer you beat, the lighter the frosting.

6/ Ice the cakes with the frosting. Either spread with a knife, or use a piping bag with a star-shaped nozzle. Decorate as desired.

STORAGE: Whipped cream cupcakes keep well for a couple of days if stored in an airtight tin in a cool place. Once iced, they should be eaten within a day.

Orange teacakes, with their multi-layer offering of sponge, fruity orange jelly filling and dark chocolate are without doubt one of the culinary highlights of childhood. What's less well known is that they are easy and a lot of fun to make at home, where you can also experiment with jelly flavours and different types of chocolate toppings, should you dare to meddle with a classic combination.

orange teacakes

FOR THE JELLY LAYER
500ml boiling water
2 x 135g packs orange jelly, broken
   into cubes

FOR THE CAKE BASES
2 eggs
60g caster sugar
60g plain flour

TO FINISH
250g dark chocolate, broken into
   pieces

YOU WILL NEED
two 12-hole nonstick muffin tins
   OR one or two flat, shallow baking
   sheets or dishes.
two baking sheets, lined with baking
   parchment

makes 20–24 cakes

1/ First make the jelly layer, allowing enough time for this to set firmly before assembling the teaakes. Pour the boiling water into a measuring jug and add the jelly cubes. Leave to melt, stirring occasionally until fully dissolved.

2/ There are two ways of making the jelly discs. To create ready-made discs, pour the jelly liquid into the bases of muffin tin moulds to make a layer 7.5mm deep (or as deep as you like). Alternatively, pour a 7.5mm layer (or any thickness you like) of jelly into 1 or 2 flat dishes or trays, and use a round cutter to create circles of jelly when set. Leave the jelly to set in the fridge until it is very firm and can be handled.

3/ While the jelly is setting, make the cake bases. Preheat the oven to 180°C (gas mark 4).

4/ Put the eggs and sugar into a large mixing bowl and whisk with an electric mixer for 4–5 minutes until pale, thick and moussey. Sift in the flour a little at a time, folding in gently with a large spoon after each addition until all the flour has been incorporated.

5/ Drop spoonfuls of the mix onto a baking sheet to make circles, leaving plenty of space between the circles. Bake in the preheated oven for 7–9 minutes until pale gold and firm to the touch. Transfer to a wire rack and leave to cool for a few minutes before carefully lifting them off the sheet. Cool completely before finishing.

6/ To finish, turn the cake bases upside down and place a disc of jelly on top. Melt the chocolate in a bowl suspended over a saucepan of just-boiled water. Line up the cake and jelly bases on a wire rack standing on a large piece of baking parchment or greaseproof paper (to catch the drips). Spoon the melted chocolate over the cakes, gently smearing it with the back of the spoon to push it to the edges. Collect any drips with a palette knife, re-melt and reuse. Leave the chocolate to set fully at room temperature before serving.

STORAGE: Orange teacakes keep well for a couple of days after making, if stored in an airtight tin in a cool but not cold place.

One of the most marvellous things about cake is that it can be baked to suit all occasions. Although an informal cuppa and a slice of simple cake round the kitchen table is one of life's great everyday delights, sometimes it is good to get out the delicate china cups and plates, a hand-embroidered vintage tablecloth and an elegant cake stand, and create something a little more formal. Make the table as pretty as a picture with your favourite flowers, lacy doilies and vintage cake forks if you have them, and bake a centrepiece cake for afternoon tea. The sort of cake that requires a little more planning and preparation, something that will look as good as it tastes, and something that will make your guests feel special. There are plenty of recipes for glorious occasion cakes because afternoon tea has been, and thankfully still is, one of the most popular and civilised events in the cake-eating world.

posh cakes

Chiffon cake can be tricky to get right as it relies on air remaining trapped in the cooked egg-white mix, and is prone to sinking. It is imperative to follow the instructions *not* to grease the tin so that the cake sticks to it, and to invert the cake the minute it comes out of the oven. The best advice is to treat it as carefully as you would a fragile soufflé, and keep it out of any draughts.

lemon chiffon cake

FOR THE CAKE

6 eggs, separated, plus 2 egg whites
230g plain flour
10g baking powder
1 teaspoon salt
300g white caster sugar (in two
    150g batches)
125ml light, mild vegetable oil
    (such as sunflower or light olive oil)
finely grated zest of 1 lemon (optional)
150ml water
1 teaspoon cream of tartar
1 teaspoon vanilla extract

FOR THE GLAZE

600g icing sugar
75g butter, melted
juice of 2–3 lemons

YOU WILL NEED

a 24cm two-piece Angel Food cake tin
(also called a 'tube tin'), OR a 24cm
round deep cake tin, ungreased

makes 1 very large cake
(serves 16–20)

1/ Preheat the oven to 160°C (gas mark 3).

2/ Put the 6 egg yolks into a small bowl, and the 8 egg whites into a bowl large enough for whisking. Sift the flour, baking powder and salt into a large mixing bowl. Add half the caster sugar and mix well to combine. Make a well in the centre and add the oil, egg yolks, lemon zest (if using) and water. Beat well with an electric mixer or wooden spoon for 1 minute until completely smooth.

3/ Whisk the egg whites until gentle peaks form. Gradually add the remaining caster sugar, the cream of tartar and the vanilla extract, whisking until the mixture is smooth, glossy and softly peaking. Spoon half the whisked egg whites into the sponge batter and fold in gently with a large metal spoon. Add the remaining egg whites and continue to fold in until combined. Pour the very light batter into the prepared tin and gently smooth the top with a spoon or spatula.

4/ Bake in the preheated oven for 50–55 minutes, by which time the cake should have risen enormously. It should be golden brown on top and is done when a metal skewer or sharp knife inserted into the centre of the cake comes out clean. Make sure you have a wire rack ready and waiting when you take the cake out of the oven.

5/ When the cake is done, remove from the oven and immediately invert the tin onto a wire rack. Leave in a warm, draught-free place to cool completely, which can take 1–2 hours. Do not touch until completely cool, then turn the cake out of the tin. Because the tin was not greased, this may be a little difficult. Run a small palette knife round the edge of the cake to loosen and gently ease the cake out of the tin. Handle with care as the sponge is very light and fluffy.

6/ To make the glaze, sift the icing sugar into a mixing bowl and add the melted butter and the juice of 2 lemons. Mix well, gradually adding more lemon juice, if needed, until you have a smooth, lightly runny glaze. With a palette knife or spatula, pour and spread the glaze over the cake, allowing it to run down the sides. Any glaze that runs off the cake can be picked up and reused. The glaze sets after about 30 minutes.

STORAGE: Lemon chiffon cake can be made a day in advance as its spongy dampness ensures it keeps well. If securely wrapped in foil and stored in a tin or cake holder in a cool place, it will be fine for 2 days after making.

variation

Orange chiffon cake: use grated orange zest instead of lemon zest, and replace some or all of the water in the sponge mix with freshly squeezed orange juice. Use orange juice instead of lemon juice in the glaze.

Battenberg cake was created in 1884 to mark the wedding of Queen Victoria's granddaughter to Prince Louis of Battenberg, with the squares representing the four princes of Battenberg. It was hugely popular in the 1960s and 1970s when it was a supermarket favourite, and its image has suffered ever since. Yet a homemade Battenberg offers a wonderful combination of soft sponge, tangy apricot jam and almondy marzipan, and is a revelation to anyone tasting it for the first time.

battenberg cake

FOR THE CAKE

175g soft butter, plus extra
  for greasing
175g caster sugar
3 eggs
a few drops of almond extract
  (optional)
150g self-raising flour
½ teaspoon baking powder
40g ground almonds
red or pink food colouring paste
200g apricot jam
icing sugar, for dusting
500g pack golden marzipan

YOU WILL NEED

one 20cm square straight-sided cake tin, greased with butter and lined with baking parchment. In order to make it easy to lift the cakes out of the tin, it's best to line it with 2 long strips of baking parchment, 20cm wide, crossed over each other. Divide the tin into 2 using a strip of foil folded over 2–3 times, with a base to help it stand up. Make sure it fits snugly, then grease with butter

*makes 1 medium–large cake
(serves 8–10)*

1/ Preheat the oven to 180°C (gas mark 4). Put the butter and sugar in a large mixing bowl. With a wooden spoon or an electric whisk, cream them together until they are pale and fluffy. Add the eggs one by one, beating well after each addition. Add the almond extract (if using).

2/ Sift the flour and baking powder into a small bowl. Add the ground almonds and stir to mix. Add the dry ingredients to the egg mixture. With a large metal spoon or flexible spatula, gently fold in until all the ingredients are combined.

3/ Divide the mixture into 2 equal parts: measure it out into 2 bowls on electronic scales (they should each weigh about 320g). Place one half on one side of the prepared tin. Colour the second half with red or pink food colouring until you have the shade of pink you like, and put this in the other half of the tin.

4/ Bake the cake in the preheated oven for 25 minutes or until a metal skewer or sharp knife inserted into the centre comes out clean. Transfer to a wire rack and leave to cool before carefully lifting or turning the 2 rectangles of sponge out of the tin. When completely cool, cut the rectangles in half lengthways and trim all four sections so that they are the same length and have straight sides and edges.

5/ Warm the apricot jam very gently in a small saucepan. Pass the jam through a sieve to remove any pieces of fruit if necessary.

6/ Lightly dust a board or worksurface and rolling pin with icing sugar. With the rolling pin, roll out the block of marzipan so that it is just over 20cm wide (or the length of your cake), then roll it out lengthways until it will fit generously around the cake (about 45cm long and 5mm thick).

7/ Brush 2 adjacent sides of each section of pink and yellow sponge and begin to assemble them in a chequerboard section in the centre of the rolled out marzipan. Brush with more jam as you go to make sure it is all held together. Beginning with what will be the base of the assembled cake, brush each side with jam and carefully wrap the marzipan round the cake, pressing it gently but firmly so that it sticks. Brush the last remaining side and overlap the marzipan on the base to make a seam. With a sharp knife, trim the marzipan and neaten the ends of the cake to tidy up the presentation. Cut into slices to serve.

STORAGE: Battenberg cake keeps well for a couple of days if stored in an airtight tin in a cool place.

Rarely does a cake have such an illustrious history, and still remain in the realms of home-baking possibility. Although some claim Sachertorte is the speciality of the Demel café in Vienna, others maintain its spiritual home is the Hotel Sacher. Genuine Sachertorte has 'Sachertorte' written with a flourish on the icing, and you can do this if you like. Alternatively, leave plain and enjoy Austrian-café style with a cloud of whipped cream.

sachertorte

FOR THE CAKE

200g dark chocolate, broken into
    small pieces
6 eggs
150g soft butter, plus extra
    for greasing
125g icing sugar
120g caster sugar
150g plain flour, sifted

FOR THE FILLING & TOPPING

6–8 tablespoons apricot jam
200g dark chocolate, broken into
    small pieces
200ml double cream
1 teaspoon glycerine
1 tablespoon icing sugar, sifted

YOU WILL NEED

a 23cm round springform cake tin,
greased with butter and base lined
with baking parchment

*makes 1 very large cake
(serves 14–16)*

1/ Preheat the oven to 160°C (gas mark 3). Melt the chocolate in a bowl sitting over a pan of just-boiled water (it will remain hot enough to melt the chocolate as long as you are patient and stir just occasionally). Remove and set aside to cool.

2/ Separate the eggs. Put the yolks in a small bowl and put the whites in a large mixing bowl. Put the butter into a second large mixing bowl and sift in the icing sugar. With a wooden spoon or electric mixer, cream until pale and smooth. Add the egg yolks one by one, beating well after each addition. Add the melted chocolate and gently fold in to mix until thoroughly combined.

3/ Whisk the egg whites until they are softly peaking. Gradually add the caster sugar a little at a time, until all the sugar has been incorporated. Now whisk well until the mix is glossy and holds its shape.

4/ With a large metal spoon or flexible spatula, spoon half the chocolate mix into the egg mix and begin to fold in gently, adding the second half when the ingredients begin to combine. Now add the flour in batches, continuing to fold until the mix is combined and has no white flecks. It should be smooth and moussey.

5/ Spoon into the prepared tin. Bake in the preheated oven for 40–45 minutes until the cake is well risen and pulling away from the sides, and a metal skewer inserted into the centre comes out clean. Transfer to a wire rack and leave to cool for 10–15 minutes before releasing from the tin. Leave to cool completely before icing.

6/ When the cake is cool, place it on a wire rack standing on a large piece of foil or greaseproof paper. Gently warm the apricot jam in a saucepan and strain it through a sieve. Slice the cake in two horizontally and fill with a layer of apricot jam. Replace the top, and brush the surface with apricot jam.

7/ To make the chocolate covering, put the chocolate in a bowl with the cream. Place the bowl over a saucepan of just-boiled water. Stir occasionally, but do not overmix as it could split. As soon as it is fully melted, remove from the heat. Add the glycerine and stir to mix, then add the icing sugar and mix again. Pour the covering over the cake, allowing it to drip down the sides. Use a palette knife to spread and neaten the icing over the top and sides. Gather up the drips and reuse if needed.

STORAGE: Sachertorte keeps well for 2 days stored in an airtight tin in a cool place.

Tres leches or 'three milk' cake is a speciality of Mexico and other South American countries, and since the 1940s it has been popular in North America and beyond. It is a sweetened milk lover's idea of heaven as it contains three milks: condensed, evaporated and fresh cream. These are mixed together and poured over the sponge, which is light and airy, and able to soak up a good proportion of the liquid while the rest forms a sweet, sticky pool of sauce. It's a large, very pale, very milky, very good cake that can be served chilled as a pudding with even more cream on top. Make this cake the day before it is needed.

tres leches cake

FOR THE CAKE
butter, for greasing
150g plain flour
1 ½ teaspoons baking powder
5 eggs, separated
200g caster sugar
80ml milk (about 5 tablespoons)
1 teaspoon vanilla extract

FOR THE SAUCE
230ml condensed milk
170ml evaporated milk
about 100ml double cream

TO FINISH
200ml double cream
maraschino or glacé cherries, to
    decorate (optional)

YOU WILL NEED
a 23cm round springform cake tin,
lightly greased with butter and base
lined with baking parchment OR a
roasting tin or Pyrex dish about
30 x 23cm, lightly greased with butter

*Makes 1 large cake
(serves 12–15 as a pudding)*

1/ Preheat the oven to 180°C (gas mark 4).
2/ Sift the flour and baking powder together into a small bowl. In a large mixing bowl, whisk the egg yolks and sugar together until very pale and creamy and doubled in size. Add the milk and vanilla extract, then add the flour mixture and gently fold in with a large spoon or flexible spatula until combined.
3/ In another large bowl, whisk the egg whites until they form soft peaks. Spoon into the cake mixture and fold in very gently and thoroughly. Spoon the mixture into the prepared baking tin or dish and level the surface with the spoon.
4/ Bake in the preheated oven for 40 minutes until well risen and golden brown on top, and a metal skewer or sharp knife inserted into the centre comes out clean. Transfer to a wire rack and leave to cool (it will deflate a little but this is normal).
5/ When the cake is cold, run a knife round the edge of the tin or dish and turn the cake out. Either invert it onto a deep serving dish that can hold the milk sauce when poured over or, if you don't have a suitable dish, invert it and return to the baking tin or dish. Pierce the surface of the cake all over with a skewer or fork.
6/ In a jug, mix the condensed milk, evaporated milk and enough double cream to bring the total liquid to 500ml. Pour over the sponge and leave to soak overnight in a cool place or in the fridge.
7/ Before serving, bring the cake to room temperature. Whip 200ml double cream so that it holds a soft peak, and spread over the top of the cake (if using). Cut into squares and top each portion with a cherry.
STORAGE: The cake is at its best the day after it has been made and allowed to soak overnight, but it will keep in the fridge for a further day or two.

Chocolate roulade is the chocolate version of the Swiss roll (see page 140), but served as a dessert because of its rich, moussey texture and cream filling. It may look challenging to make, but if you follow the instructions and stay relaxed about any cracks that appear when you roll – and they can appear quite easily no matter how carefully you try to avoid them – you will be rewarded with a deliciously indulgent-looking and indulgent-tasting cake.

chocolate roulade

FOR THE CAKE

butter, for greasing
180g good-quality chocolate
    (70% cocoa solids)
6 eggs, separated
180g caster sugar
2 tablespoons good-quality
    cocoa powder

TO FINISH

250–300ml double cream
icing sugar, for dusting

YOU WILL NEED

a Swiss roll tin, about 33 x 23cm, greased with butter and lined with baking parchment so that the parchment stands a couple of centimetres taller than the tin. Lightly grease the baking parchment

makes 1 generous roulade
(serves 6–8)

1/ Preheat the oven to 180°C (gas mark 4). Break the chocolate into pieces and put in a bowl set over a saucepan of just-boiled water. Leave to melt, stirring very occasionally. When melted, remove the bowl from the pan and leave to cool.

2/ Put the egg whites into a mixing bowl. With a hand whisk or electric whisk, whisk until softly peaking. Put the egg yolks and sugar into a second mixing bowl. With the same whisk, whisk until thick and creamy (this will take a couple of minutes). Add the melted chocolate, and with a large metal spoon or flexible spatula, gently fold in and mix until thoroughly combined.

3/ With a large metal spoon, gradually add the egg whites to the mix, a spoonful at a time, folding in carefully after each addition (the aim is to retain as much air in the mix as possible). Add the cocoa powder by sifting it into the mixture and folding in. When the mix is combined and there are no flecks of white or cocoa powder, pour it into the prepared tin and gently shake and tap the tin until the surface is level and the corners are filled.

4/ Bake in the preheated oven for 20–25 minutes until risen and the top is firm and dry. Transfer to a wire rack and leave to cool in the tin. The cake will sink and shrink a little, but this is normal. If you are making the sponge in advance, cover with a damp tea towel and leave in a cool place. It can be left overnight if necessary, but you will need to re-dampen the cloth.

5/ When it is completely cool and just before you serve it, fill and roll up the roulade. Whip the cream until it is billowing. Put a piece of baking parchment larger than the cake tin on the work surface and dust lightly with icing sugar. Invert the tin and turn the roulade out onto the paper, tugging gently at the tin's paper to bring the roulade out in one piece, then gently pull off the paper. With a sharp knife, make a shallow cut along one of the shorter ends, a couple of centimetres from the edge (this will help with the rolling up).

6/ Spread the cream over the surface of the sponge. Roll up the roulade, starting at the end with a cut and using the paper beneath to help you pull up the sponge. Handle the roulade evenly and firmly, but not too firmly or you will press out the cream. Sometimes a homemade roulade will crack as you roll, other times it just develops surface cracks. This is to be expected, and not an indication of failure.

7/ Dust generously with icing sugar and gently place with the seam underneath on a serving plate. Serve with fresh pouring or whipped cream if desired. Chocolate roulade is also delicious with fresh fruits, especially raspberries.
STORAGE: Eat as soon as possible after filling and rolling up.

It's not surprising that many baking cultures have a coconut cake; its taste and texture lend themselves to a rich, moist, sweet cake. This one is inspired by the cakes of the 1970s that were made with desiccated coconut. But if you can find shredded coconut, it will make your cakes even softer, sweeter, chewier and more coconutty.

coconut cake

FOR THE CAKE
175g soft butter, plus extra
   for greasing
3 eggs, lightly beaten
1 x 397g tin condensed milk
75g desiccated or shredded coconut
175g self-raising flour
1 level teaspoon baking powder

FOR THE ICING
450–500g icing sugar
150g soft butter
50g desiccated or shredded coconut
2–3 tablespoons milk

TO FINISH
2–3 handfuls of desiccated or
   shredded coconut

YOU WILL NEED
a 20cm round cake tin, greased with
butter and lined with baking parchment

makes 1 large cake
(serves 10–12)

1/ Preheat the oven to 160°C (gas mark 3).

2/ Put all the sponge cake ingredients into a large mixing bowl. With an electric mixer or wooden spoon, mix well until you have a smooth and light cake batter.

3/ Spoon the mixture into the prepared tin, level the surface and bake in the preheated oven for 60–70 minutes until well risen and golden brown on top, and a metal skewer or sharp knife inserted into the centre comes out clean.

4/ Transfer to a wire rack and leave to cool for 10–15 minutes before turning out of the tin. The cake is ready to ice when it is completely cool.

5/ To make the icing, sift 450g of the icing sugar into a mixing bowl and add the butter and desiccated coconut. Add a small amount of milk and mix well to combine all the ingredients into a smooth and spreadable buttercream icing. Gradually add more icing sugar and milk according to taste and if necessary to achieve a nice spreading consistency.

6/ With a large, sharp knife, cut the cake in half through the middle. Spread the lower half with one-third of the buttercream and replace the top. Now ice the sides of the cake, saving enough buttercream for the top.

7/ Cover the iced sides of the cake with desiccated coconut. Spread out a length of baking parchment cut long enough to go round the cake. Sprinkle a line of coconut a little wider than the depth of the cake along the sheet of parchment. Holding the cake carefully, roll it lightly along the line of coconut so that the sides are covered, re-rolling gently if necessary to cover any bare patches.

8/ Ice the top of the cake with the remaining buttercream and sprinkle generously with desiccated coconut.

STORAGE: Coconut cake is best eaten when fresh, but will keep for a couple of days if wrapped in foil and stored in an airtight tin in a cool place.

cook's tip
To give the buttercream icing a stronger coconut flavour, gently heat the milk with a tablespoon of desiccated coconut and leave to infuse for a few minutes before straining, cooling and using.

hazelnut meringue cake

marble bundt cake

It's surprising that a decade that produced such terrible fashions in clothes was also responsible for creating many a baked classic. The 1970s were the heyday of the hazelnut meringue cake, made with layers of nutty, chewy meringue filled with billowing cream. It looks and sounds impressive, but is remarkably straightforward to make as these particular meringues are very well-behaved, easy to handle and can be made in advance. It is particularly good when served with plenty of fresh raspberries.

hazelnut meringue cake

FOR THE CAKE
butter, for greasing
5 egg whites
280g golden caster sugar
150g finely ground hazelnuts

TO FINISH
350ml double cream
1–2 punnets fresh raspberries
icing sugar, for dusting (optional)

YOU WILL NEED
two 20cm round cake tins, lightly greased with butter and lined with baking parchment

makes 1 medium–large cake (serves 8–10)

1/ Preheat the oven to 160°C (gas mark 3).
2/ In a large mixing bowl, whisk the egg whites until softly peaking. Add the sugar in 3 or 4 batches, whisking in well after each addition, making sure you scrape down the sides of the bowl with a flexible spatula to ensure all the sugar is incorporated. Now add the hazelnuts, gently folding in until fully combined.
3/ Spoon the mixture into the prepared cake tins, dividing it equally. Bake in the preheated oven for 35–40 minutes or until pale gold and firm to the touch. Transfer to a wire rack, and leave to cool completely before carefully removing from the tins. The layers can now be stored in an airtight tin in a cool place for up to 2 days until needed.
4/ When you are ready to serve the cake, peel off any remaining baking parchment and place the bottom layer of meringue on your chosen plate or stand. Whip the cream until softly billowing (do not over-whip) and spread half over the meringue base. Add raspberries if desired. Place the second layer on top and cover with the remaining cream. Decorate with raspberries. Serve plain or with more raspberries lightly dusted with icing sugar.
STORAGE: Once the cake has been filled and covered with cream, it will start to soften so is best eaten quickly, but it does keep well for a day or so in the fridge even though some of the crispness is lost.

With its lovely swirls of light vanilla and dark chocolate sponge that make every slice different, marble cake has been a highlight of many afternoon teas. It is said to have originated in Germany in the 19th century before finding fame in America. It works well in any cake tin, but is most often baked in a Bundt tin, the tin that is closely associated with German baking. This tin is now so popular that it has become an art form in itself, with companies now making cleverly detailed versions, so you can create spectacular-looking marble cakes.

marble bundt cake

FOR THE CAKE
250g soft butter, plus extra
    for greasing
250g caster sugar
250g plain flour
2 teaspoons baking powder
4 eggs
a few drops of vanilla extract
2 tablespoons milk, plus 2 teaspoons
2 tablespoons cocoa powder
icing sugar, for dusting

YOU WILL NEED
a greased 24cm diameter ring mould with a 1.25 litre capacity (greasing is best done with a pastry brush and melted butter, especially if you are using a mould with an intricate design)

makes 1 medium–large cake (serves 8–10)

1/ Preheat the oven to 180°C (gas mark 4).
2/ Put all the ingredients except the milk and cocoa powder in a large mixing bowl and mix well with an electric whisk or wooden spoon. When thoroughly mixed, fold in the 2 tablespoons milk with a metal spoon to give a light, smooth dropping consistency.
3/ Divide the batter between 2 smaller bowls (the best way to do this is to measure it out into 2 bowls on electronic scales if you have them).
4/ Flavour one bowl with cocoa. Mix the cocoa powder with a couple of teaspoons of warm milk, then add to the mix and fold in well. You will now have one bowl of pale vanilla sponge mix, and one of dark chocolate sponge mix.
5/ Using a dessertspoon or tablespoon, drop spoonfuls of mixture into the prepared tin, alternating light and dark without making a neat pattern – go round twice, putting dollops in different places – so that when you cut you get different effects in each slice: irregular and unpredictable but a good mix of the two.
6/ Bake in the preheated oven for 35–40 minutes until a metal skewer or sharp knife comes out clean. Leave to cool on a wire rack for 5–10 minutes before turning out carefully. Leave to cool completely. If the underside is too mounded, trim to make it level. Dust with icing sugar before cutting into slices to serve.
STORAGE: Marble Bundt cake is best eaten within a day or two of making. Store in an airtight tin in a cool place.

variation
You could also drizzle the cooked cake with a thin white glacé icing made with icing sugar and water.

It would seem that few people are able to resist the devilish temptations of this large layered cake, as it is quite understandably one of the most popular baked treats in America. Despite appearances, it's deceptively light and airy due to the use of cocoa powder, rather than chocolate, and the addition of bicarbonate of soda. The sweetness of the sponge is offset by the addition of coffee (you can substitute this with milk or water if you prefer), although this is more than compensated for by the rich, sweet frosting, which is one of the distinguishing features of this delightfully sinful treat.

devil's food cake

FOR THE CAKE

125g butter, plus extra for greasing

250g caster sugar

2 eggs

225g plain flour

½ teaspoon baking powder

1 teaspoon bicarbonate of soda

50g good-quality cocoa powder

a pinch of salt

125ml cooled black coffee mixed with
    125ml milk OR a total of 250ml milk

FOR THE FROSTING

125ml milk

30g dark soft brown sugar

125g butter

300g dark chocolate, broken into
    small pieces

YOU WILL NEED

two 20cm round cake tins, greased with butter and lined with baking parchment

*makes 1 large cake
(serves 8–10)*

1/ Make the frosting first: put the milk, sugar and butter in a saucepan and heat gently until the butter has melted and the sugar has dissolved. Take off the heat, add the pieces of chocolate and leave to melt, swirling the pan occasionally. When melted, whisk well until smooth and glossy. Leave to cool for 60–70 minutes, by which time the frosting will have changed consistency and become thick and fudgy.

2/ To make the cake: preheat the oven to 180°C (gas mark 4). Put the butter and sugar in a large mixing bowl. With a wooden spoon or an electric whisk, cream them together until they are pale and fluffy. Add the eggs one by one, beating well after each addition.

3/ Measure out the flour, baking powder, bicarbonate of soda, cocoa powder and salt into a small bowl. Measure out the coffee and milk in a jug. Add half the dry ingredients to the mixing bowl and fold in with a large metal spoon. Add half the liquid and mix in gently. Now add the remaining ingredients and fold in thoroughly until well combined.

4/ Divide the mixture equally between the 2 prepared tins, level the surfaces and bake in the preheated oven for 25 minutes. The cakes are ready when a metal skewer or sharp knife inserted into the centre of the cake comes out clean. Transfer to a wire rack and leave to cool completely before icing.

5/ When the layers are ready to ice, place one of them upside down (to give a flat surface) on a cake stand, plate or icing stand. With a palette knife, spread one-third of the chocolate frosting over the surface. Place the other layer on top, the right way up. Spread frosting over the top and sides using a swirling motion.

6/ Keep in a cool place until you are ready to serve the cake, as the frosting melts quite quickly in warm temperatures.

STORAGE: This cake is best eaten on the day of making, although it will be fine the following day if kept in a cool, dark place.

cook's tip

If you plan to serve the cake soon after making, make the frosting first as it requires time to cool before spreading.

The 1960s and 1970s were topsy-turvy times, and it seemed some cakes followed suit. These were the decades in which upside-down fruit cakes were fashionable, and none more so than the often garishly colourful upside-down pineapple cake. It may be a throwback to an era of psychedelia and tinned fruit, but it's an iconic retro cake that does at least have a great taste to match its appearance. It's worth using tinned pineapple in juice (rather than syrup) for extra flavour.

upside-down pineapple cake

FOR THE CAKE
175g soft butter, plus extra for greasing
25g caster sugar
6–8 tinned pineapple rings in fruit juice (not syrup)
8–16 whole glacé cherries (optional)
175g light soft brown sugar
3 eggs, lightly beaten
200g self-raising flour
2 tablespoons pineapple juice from the tin

FOR THE SYRUP
100ml pineapple juice from the tin
50g caster sugar

YOU WILL NEED
the ideal tin for this cake is an all-in-one baking tin, such as a metal tart tin without a loose base, which ensures the juices and liquids won't run out and burn during baking. A shallow metal pie tin or Tarte Tatin tin with slightly sloping sides is perfect. The one used here measures about 24cm wide at the top and 20cm wide across the base. Alternatively, use a 23cm round loose-bottom or springform tin

makes 1 large cake
(serves 8–10)

1/ Preheat the oven to 180°C (gas mark 4). Grease the tin generously and sprinkle 25g caster sugar over the base.

2/ Drain the pineapple rings, reserving the juice, and arrange them close together in the tin. Place a glacé cherry in the centre of each ring (if using), and, if you wish, make a pretty pattern in the spaces between the rings with more cherries.

3/ Now make the sponge. Put the butter and brown sugar in a large mixing bowl. With a wooden spoon or an electric whisk, cream them together until they are pale and fluffy. Add the eggs one by one, beating well after each addition.

4/ Sift in the flour, add 2 tablespoons of the pineapple juice and fold in gently with a metal spoon until all the ingredients are thoroughly combined.

5/ Carefully spoon the mixture over the pineapple rings in the tin, level the surface with the back of the spoon, and bake in the preheated oven for 40 minutes or until a metal skewer or sharp knife inserted into the centre of the cake comes out clean. Leave the cake in its tin on a wire rack to cool for a few minutes.

6/ While you are waiting, make a syrup by putting the pineapple juice and caster sugar in a saucepan and boiling over a medium heat, without stirring, until it thickens – this takes a few minutes. Remove from the heat.

7/ The next step is to turn the cake out of the tin so that it is upside down on a plate or cake stand. Ease a sharp knife round the edge of the cake to loosen it. The easiest way to get it out in one whole piece is to place the plate or stand over the tin, then, wearing oven gloves and holding the tin and plate together, quickly invert both the tin and the plate/stand so the plate is the right way up and the tin is upside down on it. Leave for a few moments, give it a little shake to nudge the cake out, then carefully lift off the tin. The cake should now be upside down, intact, on the plate.

8/ Spoon the syrup evenly over the surface, using as much as you think necessary. Leave to cool before serving with cream or custard if desired.

STORAGE: Upside-down pineapple cake is at its best on the day of making and although it will still taste fine the next day, it will have lost some of its initial gloss and good looks.

It's easy to create a classic German *Kaffee-und-Küchen* (coffee-and-cake) moment with this featherlight sponge filled with cream and slices of ripe fruit. The semolina (*gries* in German) gives ultra-airy results with a barely discernible crunch that contrasts beautifully with the rich cream and luscious fruit. It's a well-behaved sponge that can be made a couple of days in advance, then simply and easily filled with slices of pear, peach or any ripe fruit in season, just before you get out the pretty china (vintage Thomas china from Bavaria would be the ideal and authentic choice) and share in one of the most civilised, European cake traditions.

griestorte with pears

FOR THE CAKE
butter, for greasing
3 eggs
120g caster sugar
juice of ¹/₂ a lemon
60g fine semolina
20g ground almonds

TO FINISH
150–200ml double cream
3–4 ripe pears or peaches
icing sugar, for dusting

YOU WILL NEED
a 20cm round cake tin, lightly greased with butter and lined with baking parchment

makes 1 medium–large cake (serves 8–10)

1/ Preheat the oven to 180°C (gas mark 4).
2/ Separate the eggs and put the egg whites in a mixing bowl, and the yolks in a separate mixing bowl.
3/ Add the caster sugar to the egg yolks and with a whisk or electric mixer, whisk until pale and creamy. Add the lemon juice and whisk again. Add the semolina and ground almonds and fold in with a large wooden spoon or flexible spatula.
4/ Whisk the eggs whites until softly peaking. Spoon into the yolk and sugar mixture. Fold in gently with a large metal spoon or flexible spatula until all the ingredients are fully combined.
5/ Spoon into the prepared tin, level the surface and bake in the preheated oven for 30 minutes until well risen, golden brown and firm to the touch on top. Transfer to a wire rack and leave to cool before turning out of the tin. You can now store the cake in an airtight tin in a cool place for up to 2 days before filling.
6/ When the cake has cooled completely, you can fill and finish it. With a sharp knife, cut the cake horizontally into 2 layers. Place the bottom layer on your chosen cake plate or stand.

7/ Whip the cream (adjust the quantity according to how rich and creamy you like your cakes) until it is light and billowing, but do not over-whip. With a palette knife, spread half the cream over the bottom layer of sponge. Peel and slice the fruit and place it in a layer on top of the cream. Gently spread the remaining cream over the fruit, replace the top layer of sponge, and dust with icing sugar.
STORAGE: Griestorte sponge is at its lightest on the day of making but it keeps well for up to 2 days before filling. Once the cake has been filled, it should be eaten soon after, preferably on the same day, although it will keep until the next day if stored in the fridge.

The full name of this cake, *Schwarzwälder Kirschtorte*, explains that it is flavoured with kirsch from the Black Forest region of Germany. Although written histories prove it has been around since the 1930s, it was in the 1970s that it became the dessert cake of choice. It's a heady mix of chocolate sponge, alcohol, cherries and cream that will be forever linked to platform shoes as tall as the cake.

black forest gateau

FOR THE CAKE

175g soft butter, plus extra
for greasing
175g caster sugar
5 eggs, separated
125g self-raising flour
75g cocoa powder

FOR THE FILLING & TOPPING

1 x 390g jar of black cherries with
kirsch, or 250g (drained weight) of
tinned black cherries
2–3 tablespoons kirsch (or liquid from
the jar of cherries, if using)
350ml double cream
grated chocolate or chocolate swirls
(optional)

YOU WILL NEED

three 20cm round shallow cake tins,
greased with butter and bases lined
with baking parchment

makes 1 large cake
(serves 12)

1/ Preheat the oven to 180°C (gas mark 4).
2/ Put the butter and sugar in a large mixing bowl. With a wooden spoon or an electric whisk, cream them together until they are pale and fluffy. Add the egg yolks one by one, beating well after each addition.
3/ In a separate, clean bowl, whisk the egg whites until they are softly peaking. Sift the flour and cocoa powder together onto a plate. With a metal spoon or flexible spatula, gradually add the egg whites and slide in the sifted flour mix to the butter, sugar and egg mix. Fold in gently after each addition until thoroughly and evenly combined, and no flecks of white remain.
4/ Divide the mixture equally between 3 tins and level the surfaces. Bake in the preheated oven for 15–20 minutes until a fine toothpick or metal skewer inserted into the centre of a cake comes out clean. Transfer to a wire rack and leave to cool before turning out of the tins and peeling off the papers. Make sure the cakes are completely cool before filling and decorating.
5/ Drain the cherries retaining the liquid. Sprinkle the kirsch or cherry liquor over the surface of each layer of cake. Whip the cream until softly billowing, but do not over-whip. Place the first layer of sponge upside down on a plate or stand. With a palette knife or spatula, spread a layer of cream on top. Dot a third of the cherries over the surface. Place the second layer of sponge, also upside down, on top and repeat with the cream and cherries. Finally, place the third layer on top, the right way up, and cover with the remaining cream. Either create a circle of cherries on top, or heap them in the middle. Add a grating of dark chocolate if desired. Serve as soon as possible after filling and decorating.
STORAGE: Although the sponge layers will freeze well for up to a month or keep for a couple of days in airtight tins in a cool place, once the cream and cherries have been added, the cake should be eaten quickly.

It's not clear whether the Swiss really did invent the Swiss roll, or whether it is in fact simply a name coined for a style of cake that is made in many countries around the world. However, the name stuck, and for many it evokes memories of childhood teas, school dinners and afternoons with aunties. The sponge is light and very rollable as it contains a high proportion of whisked eggs and sugar, but no butter. It can be filled with jam, fruit curd, cream or buttercream, and is still one of the great home-baked treats that puts shop-bought versions to shame. It does not keep well and should be eaten on the day of making while it is still fluffy and airy.

swiss roll

FOR THE CAKE
butter, for greasing
3 large eggs
80g caster sugar, plus extra
    for dredging
80g plain flour, plus extra for dusting
a pinch of salt
your chosen filling – jam, orange or
    lemon curd (see opposite),
    fresh whipped cream
icing sugar, for dusting (optional)

YOU WILL NEED
a 30 x 20cm Swiss roll tin or a similar flat baking tin. Grease the tin with butter and line with baking parchment, making sure the lining stands a couple of centimetres taller than the tin. Grease the parchment and dust lightly with flour to prevent the sponge sticking

makes 1 medium Swiss roll
(serves 6)

1/ Preheat the oven to 190°C (gas mark 5).
2/ Put the eggs and sugar into a large mixing bowl or the bowl of an electric mixer. Whisk nonstop at full speed for 5 minutes, by which time the mixture will be very pale and creamy and 3 times its original volume. If whisking by hand, mix until you achieve the same results.
3/ Measure the flour into a bowl, add the pinch of salt and sift over the mixture, a small amount at a time. After each addition, fold the flour in very carefully and gently with a large metal spoon, working in a figure of 8 motion. Make sure all the flour has been incorporated.
4/ Spoon the mixture into the prepared tin. Shake the tin lightly to ensure the sponge mixture is even and reaches all the corners. Avoid pressing with the spoon if possible as this removes precious air bubbles.
5/ Bake in the oven for 10–12 minutes or until the sponge turns pale gold and is springy to the touch. Do not overcook.
6/ While the sponge is in the oven, cut a piece or strip of baking parchment 2–3cm larger on all sides than the base of your tin. Place on a work surface and dredge evenly with caster sugar; this will stop the sponge sticking while it cools and contributes to the classic, lightly sugary Swiss roll exterior.
7/ Remove the tin from the oven, and immediately invert the sponge onto the sugared parchment. Starting from a short end, lift the parchment and carefully roll up the sponge with the parchment still inside to form a neat roll, and leave to cool.
8/ When the cake has cooled completely, carefully unroll and remove the baking parchment from the surface. Spread with your chosen filling and re-roll, pulling away gently from the sugar-dredged parchment beneath. Dust liberally with icing or caster sugar, if desired.
STORAGE: Serve fresh and on the day of making – homemade Swiss roll does not keep well.

FOR THE FILLING

3–4 lemons, to give about 200ml juice (room temperature lemons yield more juice than lemons straight from the fridge)

4 eggs, plus 3 egg yolks

300g caster sugar

200g butter

makes 3 x 350g jars

filling variation: lemon curd

The old saying 'When life gives you lemons, make lemonade' could be altered to, 'When life gives you egg yolks, make lemon curd', because when you are baking vintage cakes (for example Meringues, page 158 or Chiffon Cake, page 120), you are likely to find yourself with leftover yolks, and lemon curd is the perfect way to make something with them that can be used in and on future cakes. Real, homemade lemon curd is wonderful on bread and butter, in scones, Swiss rolls, éclairs, sweet buns and fairy cakes, and an excellent alternative to jam in a Victoria sandwich cake. It's not difficult, and you can make a few jars with little effort and fuss in less than 15 minutes – as long as you give it your undivided attention when it's cooking. This recipe omits the zest as it can create a touch of bitterness, and to make it even smoother it pays to strain the just-cooked curd through a fine sieve.

First make sure your jars are absolutely clean. It's not vital to sterilise them as you will be keeping the lemon curd in the fridge and it doesn't last very long, but a wash in very hot water or in a dishwasher is necessary. Leave to dry rather than drying with a tea towel, or dry in a low oven for a few minutes.

1/ Squeeze the lemons to obtain the juice.

2/ Put the eggs, egg yolks and sugar in a mixing bowl. With a metal whisk, mix well to combine thoroughly until the sugar has dissolved.

3/ Pour the eggs and sugar mix into a large, heavy-based saucepan and add the butter. Over a low heat, gently warm the mix, whisking frequently. Once the butter has melted, cook very gently, stirring all the time with a wooden spoon or flexible spatula to prevent lumps of egg white forming. The mixture will thicken and have the consistency of custard. This will take just a few minutes. Once you have a smooth, thick curd, remove the pan from the heat.

4/ While still hot, strain through a sieve into a clean bowl with a lip or a large jug. Pour into clean jars straightaway. Seal, or just screw on the lids. Leave to cool and keep in the fridge until needed. STORAGE: Lemon curd will keep for a couple of weeks in the fridge.

'Mocha' sounds so sophisticated and grown-up, with its suggestion of dark, roasted coffee beans and little cups of coffee with chocolate served in chic European cafés. The mix of flavours, both dark and bitter, has a fine vintage pedigree and has been used to make impressively fine-tasting cakes for decades. However, it's a mistake to think that mocha cake is only for the adults, as it's surprisingly popular with younger cake-fanciers.

mocha cake

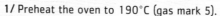

FOR THE CAKE
180g butter
180g self-raising flour
50g good-quality cocoa powder
225g light soft brown sugar
100ml strong coffee, cooled
4 eggs, separated
1 chocolate flake (or use grated chocolate), to decorate

FOR THE ICING
400–450g icing sugar
150g soft butter
2–4 tablespoons cold strong coffee

YOU WILL NEED
a 20cm round deep cake tin, greased with butter and lined with baking parchment

makes 1 medium–large cake (serves 8–10)

1/ Preheat the oven to 190°C (gas mark 5).
2/ Melt the butter in a saucepan and leave to cool. Sift the flour and cocoa powder into a large mixing bowl. Add the sugar and stir to mix.
3/ When the butter is cool, add the coffee and egg yolks. Whisk or beat well until smooth. In a separate bowl, whisk the eggs whites until they are softly peaking.
4/ Pour the contents of the saucepan into the bowl containing the flour, cocoa powder and sugar. Mix well with a spatula or wooden spoon until thoroughly combined. Now add the whisked egg whites in several batches, folding in gently with a large metal spoon. Continue folding in until no white flecks remain. Spoon the mix into the prepared tin, and level the surface with the back of the spoon.
5/ Bake for 30 minutes, then reduce the oven temperature to 160°C (gas mark 3) and bake for a further 20–25 minutes until the cake is well risen and springy to the touch, and a metal skewer or sharp knife inserted into the centre comes out clean. Transfer to a wire rack and leave to cool for 15 minutes before turning out of the tin. The cake is ready to ice when it has cooled completely.
6/ To make the icing, sift 400g icing sugar into a large mixing bowl and add the soft butter. Gradually add the strong coffee according to taste (you can also use stronger/weaker coffee depending on your preference). Mix well with a wooden spoon or flexible spatula until you have a smooth, spreadable buttercream, adding more icing sugar if necessary to get a pleasing consistency.
7/ With a sharp knife, cut the cake in half horizontally. Spread half the buttercream over the surface of the lower layer. Replace the top layer, and spread the remaining buttercream over the top of the cake. Decorate with a crushed flake or grated chocolate if you prefer.
STORAGE: Mocha cake is delicious on the day it is made, and keeps well for a couple of days if wrapped in foil and stored in a cool place.

Strawberry shortcake is a classic American dessert cake, with an unbroken history of appearances in vintage recipe books, and it remains as popular as ever today. It's a celebration of the strawberry, and is best made in season when the fruits are juicy, ripe and full of flavour. The shortcake is a simple, airy, crumbly layer which soaks up the juices, and should always be eaten as fresh as possible.

strawberry shortcake

FOR THE CAKES
325g plain flour, plus extra for dusting
½ teaspoon salt
4 teaspoons baking powder
100g caster sugar
125g cold butter, cubed
up to 150ml single or double cream
1 egg, lightly beaten

FOR THE TOPPING
1 punnet fresh strawberries
  (see cook's tip)
1–2 tablespoons caster sugar
250ml double cream

YOU WILL NEED
1 baking sheet, lined with baking parchment

makes 14–16 square shortcakes

cook's tip
Prepare the strawberries 1 hour in advance of serving them (but no longer as they start to go mushy after a while).

1/ Preheat the oven to 200°C (gas mark 6).

2/ First prepare the strawberries for the topping. Rinse if necessary and slice into halves or quarters, depending on size. Place in a small bowl and sprinkle with 1–2 tablespoons caster sugar according to taste and the sweetness of the fruit. Gently stir or tumble the fruit with your hands so that it is coated with sugar. Cover, and leave to macerate for 1 hour, by which time the strawberries will have softened and a sweet juice will have formed.

3/ Make the shortcakes. Put the flour, salt, baking powder and sugar into a large mixing bowl and stir to mix.

4/ Add the cold, cubed butter and rub into the dry ingredients using your fingertips, until the mixture looks like fine sandy breadcrumbs.

5/ Measure 125ml of the cream into a jug, add the beaten egg and mix well. Pour into the bowl and mix with a fork, bringing the ingredients together to make a soft, slightly sticky dough. Add a little more cream if necessary if the mix is too dry.

6/ Work into a ball and place on a floured surface. With a floured rolling pin, quickly and gently roll out the dough until smooth and about 1cm thick. Cut into 14–16 squares (or rectangles or circles), re-rolling the trimmings until all the dough has been used.

7/ Place the squares on the prepared baking sheet with enough space between them to allow for expansion. Bake in the preheated oven for 10–15 minutes until well risen and pale golden brown.

8/ Remove from the oven and transfer to a wire rack to cool completely.

9/ When you are ready to serve the shortcakes, whip the double cream until it is softly billowing (don't over-whip as it stiffens very quickly). Spread each shortcake liberally with the whipped cream, top with the strawberries and spoon the juices over the fruit. Serve 'open' like this, or alternatively, place a second shortcake on top to serve in the classic way.

STORAGE: Strawberry shortcake should be eaten on the day of making. Serve as soon as the cream and strawberries have been added.

The exact history of this cake is not clear, but Queen Victoria herself apparently enjoyed little 'silver' and 'gold' sponge cakes made using egg whites and egg yolks respectively. The mixes can be used to make individual cakes (they look particularly pretty in silver and gold cake cases) or, as here, they can be swirled together to create a subtle marbled effect. The cake would make a lovely centrepiece for a special anniversary celebration.

silver & gold cake

FOR THE SILVER CAKE

120g lard or soft butter
120g white caster sugar
3 egg whites
a few drops almond extract (optional)
120g self-raising flour
50g ground almonds

FOR THE GOLD CAKE

120g soft butter
120g golden caster sugar
3 egg yolks
120g self-raising flour
½ teaspoon baking powder
1–2 tablespoons milk

TO FINISH

250g golden marzipan OR
   ready-to-roll icing
1–2 tablespoons apricot jam
yellow food colouring paste (optional)
icing sugar, to dust

YOU WILL NEED

a paper doily and icing sugar, to dust
a 20cm round cake tin, greased and
   base lined with baking parchment
2 large mixing bowls as this cake is
   made with 2 sponges

*makes 1 medium-large cake
(serves 8–10)*

1/ Preheat the oven to 180°C (gas mark 4).

2/ Make the silver part of the cake: put the lard or butter and sugar into a large mixing bowl and cream with a wooden spoon or electric mixer until well mixed. In a separate bowl, whisk the eggs whites until softly peaking. Spoon into the fat and sugar mixture along with a few drops of almond extract (if using), and gently fold in with a metal spoon. Sift in the flour and almonds, and continue to fold in until all the ingredients are combined and you have a light, smooth cake mix. Set aside.

3/ Make the gold part of the cake: put the butter and sugar in the second mixing bowl, and cream until light and smooth. Add the egg yolks and beat well to combine. Sift in the flour and baking powder and add a tablespoon of milk. With a large metal spoon or flexible spatula, gently fold in to combine the ingredients, adding a little more milk if necessary to obtain a smooth consistency.

4/ With a tablespoon, spoon the 2 sponge mixes into the tin, alternating silver and gold spoonfuls and placing the spoonfuls so that you make a good pattern with the two colours. When all the mix has been added, gently smooth the top with the back of the spoon. Bake in the preheated oven for 45–50 minutes until well risen and a metal skewer or sharp knife inserted into the centre comes out clean. Transfer to a wire rack and leave to cool for 10 minutes before turning out of the tin. Leave to cool completely before covering.

5/ To cover the cake with marzipan or ready-to-roll icing, first make the surface of the cake level by slicing off the bump of sponge on top. Brush lightly with warmed apricot jam. If using ready-to-roll icing, colour first (if desired) with a little yellow food colouring paste. Lightly dust your work surface with icing sugar and roll out the marzipan or icing to form a circle a little larger than the cake – use the base of the 20cm round cake tin as a size guide. Gently press the tin base onto the marzipan or icing and with a sharp knife cut round the edge to make a disc. Place the disc on top of the cake.

6/ To make the pattern on top, put a paper doily on the cake and sift icing sugar evenly and generously over the doily. Remove the doily carefully.

STORAGE: This cake keeps well for up to 2 days if stored in a tin in a cool place.

In the world of vintage baking, one thing is very clear: a cake should never be judged on its looks, as the plainest offering can often turn out to be heart-stoppingly good. Yet there are also some fabulous fancy and frivolous cakes in pretty colours and shapes that woo us with their appearance and deliver a little mouthful of delicious indulgence. These are the treats you find beautifully, artistically and far too temptingly arranged in smart cake shops and pâtisseries; treats that are triumphs of daintiness and, seemingly, the province of the professional cake-maker. But this isn't true; previous generations of home-bakers, who would never have countenanced buying cake from shops, knew that many fancies and frivolities can be made successfully and easily in any domestic kitchen. Although the recipes here are very straightforward, it's hard not to bask in a sense of achievement in making such charming little treats that are more usually purchased. So muster your confidence, take your time and turn out a plateful of rich, boozy buns and sweet, honeyed madeleines or creamy éclairs that will bring delight to any sweet-toothed cake-lover.

fancies & frivolities

Fondant fancies are glossy, dainty squares that are the epitome of afternoon tea and pâtisserie poshness, and should undoubtedly be served with pretty doilies and floral bone china to complete the effect. They are a lot easier to make than you may imagine, and at home you are not obliged to use ladylike pastel shades. They add a touch of glamour and style to any party or celebration, and the colours and decoration can be adapted to suit the occasion.

fondant fancies

FOR THE CAKES
180g soft butter
180g caster sugar
3 eggs
180g self-raising flour
a few drops of vanilla extract
1–2 tablespoons milk, to mix

FOR THE FILLING
75g soft butter
200g icing sugar
a few drops of vanilla extract
1–2 tablespoons milk, to mix

FOR THE ICING
700–800g fondant icing sugar
cold water, to mix
food colouring pastes

YOU WILL NEED
a 20cm square tin, lightly greased with butter and base lined with baking parchment

makes 20–25 fancies

1/ Preheat the oven to 180°C (gas mark 4). Put the butter and sugar in a large mixing bowl. With a wooden spoon or an electric whisk, cream them together until they are pale and fluffy. Add the eggs one by one, beating well each time.
2/ Add the flour, vanilla extract and a tablespoon of milk. With a large metal spoon or flexible spatula, fold in until you have a smooth mix, adding a little more milk if necessary to get a soft dropping consistency. Spoon the mixture into the cake tin and smooth the surface with the back of the spoon or spatula. Bake in the preheated oven for 35–40 minutes until well risen, golden brown, and a metal skewer or sharp knife inserted into the centre of the cake comes out clean.
3/ Transfer to a wire rack and leave to cool for a few minutes before turning out. Leave to cool completely, then trim the cake so that the edges and corners are neat, and carefully level the top. Cut the cake in half horizontally.
4/ Make the filling: put the butter in a bowl and sift in the icing sugar. Add the vanilla and 1 tablespoon milk. Mix well until you have a smooth, spreadable consistency, adding a little more milk if necessary. Spread the buttercream filling over the bottom layer of sponge and replace the top. With a sharp knife, cut the cake into 4 x 4 or 5 x 5 squares to make 16 or 25 cubes. Turn these upside down so that the sharpest corners are uppermost, and place well apart on a wire rack.
5/ To make the fondant icing, sift 700g fondant icing sugar into a large mixing bowl. Add a few drops of water at a time until you get a smooth icing that is thick enough to drip slowly from a spoon. Divide into 2 or more smaller bowls, depending on how many colours you want to use. With a toothpick, add a small amount of food colouring paste to each bowl and mix well.
6/ Place the wire rack on one side of a piece of baking parchment, which is twice the length of the rack. Ice the cakes by holding a spoonful of icing just above each cake, moving the spoon around to cover the corners and to encourage the icing to drip down the sides. Deal with a batch of cakes this way, then move the rack to the other half of the baking parchment so that you can scoop up the icing drips and reuse. Spoon more icing over any uncovered areas of the sponge cakes, using a wet finger help spread it. Once covered, leave the cakes to dry for 30 minutes before piping or spoon-drizzling lines of icing over the top.
STORAGE: Fondant fancies keep well for up to 2 days after making, stored in a tin.

French macaroons (*macarons*) were popular in France long before the Parisian company Ladurée sandwiched two shells together with a sweet filling, creating the ultimate tea-salon fancy. Lately, macaroons have become a sophisticated treat, with pâtissiers vying to outdo one another with their creativity. As a result, macaroons are often viewed as difficult to make at home, which isn't true; you just need to take your time, follow the instructions and not worry about perfect results.

macaroons

FOR THE SHELLS
125g finely ground almonds
175g icing sugar
3 large egg whites
75g caster sugar
food colouring paste (optional)

SUGGESTED FILLINGS
macaroons can be filled in a variety of ways. Whipped cream with or without a little jam or fruit curd is a quick and easy filling. Alternatively, use a light buttercream (see below) or ganache (the topping on the Boston Cream Pie on page 165 would work well)

FOR THE FILLING
120–150g icing sugar
60–75g soft butter
flavouring, such as a little very strong
    cold coffee, a few drops of vanilla
    extract, or 1–2 dessertspoons
    lemon or orange curd

YOU WILL NEED
2 or 3 baking sheets, lined with baking
    parchment
a piping bag with 1cm plain nozzle
    OR medium-sized sealable plastic
    food bag

makes 30–40 shells, depending on size (15–20 macaroons when sandwiched together)

1/ Start by preparing the baking sheets. Line with baking parchment and, depending on the size of macaroon you want to make, and allowing for the fact they will expand, draw circles 3–4cm in diameter well apart on the sheets (such as 12 circles per sheet). Make sure the circles can be seen when the baking parchment is turned over, because if you pipe directly onto the drawn lines, the macaroons will pick up the markings.

2/ Prepare a piping bag with plain, 1cm nozzle. If you don't have a piping bag, it is possible to pipe macaroons from a plastic food bag with one of the corners snipped off. Place your piping bag in a jug to make it easier to fill with mixture.

3/ If possible, grind the ground almonds in batches with the icing sugar until very fine. (This makes a huge difference to the smoothness of the mixture as many commercially ground almonds are not fine enough.) Sift the icing sugar and ground almonds into a large mixing bowl.

4/ In a separate, clean bowl, whisk the egg whites until they form soft peaks. Add the caster sugar in 3–4 batches, whisking well after each addition until you have a glossy, satiny mix. If you are colouring your macaroons with food colouring paste, use a toothpick to add a small amount at this point until you get the shade you like. Spoon into the bowl holding the sugar and almonds.

5/ With a large metal spoon or flexible spatula, fold in gently until the mixture has a thick, smooth, creamy consistency. If you stop too soon, while there are still bubbles in the mix, you will have grainy-textured macaroons.

6/ Spoon the mix into the piping bag and pipe into circles on the prepared baking sheets. After piping, lift each sheet and, keeping it level, bring it down sharply on the work surface a couple of times in order to dislodge any bubbles of trapped air. Now leave the macaroons at room temperature for 20–30 minutes to form a 'skin'. They are ready to go in the oven when you can touch them very lightly without any mix sticking to your fingertip. While the macaroons are sitting, preheat the oven to 160°C (gas mark 3).

7/ When ready, bake in the preheated oven for 10–15 minutes until the macaroons have risen and are firm and dry on top: exact timing will depend on the size of your macaroons (10–12 minutes for 3cm and 12–15 minutes for 4cm). Transfer to a wire rack to cool. When cool, carefully lift off the paper with a palette knife or fish slice. At this point, the macaroons can be stored in an airtight tin in a cool place for several days if necessary.

8/ When you are ready to serve them, make the filling. Sift 120g of the icing sugar into a mixing bowl and add 60g of the butter. Mix well, adding more butter or icing sugar according to taste. Add your chosen flavouring, and a little milk if necessary to give a smooth, spreadable consistency (milk won't be necessary if you are using lemon curd).

9/ Sandwich the shells together with the filling. Use a knife to spread the filling on one shell. Place the second shell on top and very gently push down and twist the top a little to give a smooth edge to the filling.

STORAGE: Once filled, macaroons keep well for a couple of days in the fridge, but they should be brought up to room temperature before serving.

french madeleines

english madeleines

The French madeleine is one of the world's most famous cakes, forever associated with Proust, the town of Commercy (which is the centre of commercial madeleine production), and its distinctive scallop shape formed by the special baking tin. The recipe calls for the sponge mixture to have two periods of 'resting time' and it really is worth allowing for these as they make an enormous difference to the taste and texture.

french madeleines

FOR THE CAKES

125g butter, plus extra for greasing
100g icing sugar, plus extra for dusting
40g ground almonds
40g plain flour, plus extra for dusting
3 egg whites
1–2 teaspoons clear, runny honey
½ teaspoon salt
grated zest of ½ a lemon (optional)

YOU WILL NEED

a madeleine tin (to make
10–12 madeleines)

*makes 10–12 madeleines
(depending on the size of the
madeleine tin moulds)*

cook's tip

*Allow 2 hours for making if
you are planning to serve the
madeleines ultra-fresh. Most
of this is resting time in the
fridge, not making time.*

1/ Begin by making a simple beurre noisette, which will give a subtle nutty flavour. Melt the butter in a heavy-based saucepan over a medium heat until it starts to boil. Sizzle gently for 2–3 minutes until it has darkened slightly in colour and has a nice nutty scent. Do not let it turn dark brown and burn. Strain through a fine sieve and set aside to cool.

2/ Sift the icing sugar, ground almonds and flour into a medium-sized bowl (one that can fit into the fridge). Using a fork, whisk the egg whites into the dry mix. Next, add the honey and continue to whisk. Pour in the beurre noisette (which should be warm, not hot), add the salt and lemon zest and mix well.

3/ Cover the bowl tightly with clingfilm and leave the mixture to rest in the fridge for 1 hour (longer will not hurt it).

4/ Prepare the madeleine tin. It is worth making the effort as this prevents the madeleines sticking and makes it easier to remove them from the mould when they are cool without spoiling the pretty ridges and shape. With a pastry brush, grease each mould with melted butter. Now lightly dust them with flour by sifting a little over the moulds, tapping the sheet gently and tipping out any excess flour.

5/ Spoon the mixture into the moulds, filling each one to just under the level of the tin and return to the fridge for 30 minutes to rest again. While the madeleines are resting, preheat the oven to 160°C (gas mark 3).

6/ Bake in the preheated oven for 10–15 minutes or until well risen, visibly cooked in the centre, yellow-gold in the middle and brown round the edges. Transfer to a wire rack. Leave to cool for a few minutes before turning out of the tin. Dust lightly with icing sugar, and eat while fresh and warm.

STORAGE: Homemade madeleines are at their best on the day of making, but taste fine the next day – just not as good.

The French madeleine might bring back spiritual, Proustian memories of lost time, but just one look at a tray of English madeleines will evoke memories of childhood and visits to local bakeries that proudly displayed their different dainties and fancies on certain days of the week. They are a real blast from the past, and a delight to make at home, where children will enjoy getting their fingers sticky before discovering the taste of an old-fashioned treat. English madeleines get their tall, flat-topped, conical shape from dariole moulds, but can just as easily be baked in deep muffin tins or little pudding bowls.

english madeleines

FOR THE CAKES
130g soft butter
130g caster sugar
2 eggs
a few drops of vanilla extract (optional)
130g self-raising flour
scant ½ teaspoon baking powder
1–2 tablespoons milk, to mix

TO FINISH
3–4 tablespoons seedless raspberry
    jam (or any red jam)
desiccated coconut (about 80g or a
    couple of handfuls)

TO DECORATE
half a glacé cherry and, if available,
a candied angelica leaf or two
per madeleine

YOU WILL NEED
a few dariole moulds or pudding
    moulds, greased with butter (the
    madeleines shown were made in
    dariole moulds measuring 6.25cm
    high, 5.5cm across the top and 4cm
    across the base)
1 baking sheet

*makes 9–12 madeleines
(depending on the size of
the moulds)*

1/ Line the base of each mould with a small disc of baking parchment. Preheat the oven to 180°C (gas mark 4).

2/ Put the butter and sugar in a large mixing bowl. With a wooden spoon or an electric whisk, cream them together until they are pale and fluffy. Add the eggs one by one, and a few drops of vanilla extract (if using), beating well each time.

3/ Sift in the flour and baking powder and fold in gently with a large metal spoon. Add 1 tablespoon of milk to give a soft dropping consistency, or more if needed.

4/ Spoon the mixture into the moulds, filling each one about two-thirds full. Place the moulds on a baking sheet, and bake in the preheated oven for 15 minutes or until well risen and golden brown.

5/ Transfer to a wire rack and leave to cool until the moulds can be handled with ease. Gently turn the cakes out of the moulds and remove the parchment. Stand upright and leave to cool completely. Make a second batch if there is mixture leftover.

6/ When the cakes are completely cool, trim the bases so that they are flat, and the cakes can stand upright and are all more or less the same height.

7/ Put the jam in a saucepan and warm very gently over a low heat until it has melted. If you do not have seedless jam, pass the jam through a sieve at this point to remove seeds and pulp. Spread a handful or so of desiccated coconut onto a plate or board.

8/ With a pastry brush, glaze the madeleines with warm jam. Gently roll each one in the coconut to cover. Stand upright on a cake plate or stand, and decorate each one with half a glacé cherry and an angelica leaf or two (if using).

STORAGE: Eat within a day or two and store in an airtight tin in a cool place.

cook's tip
*If you don't have enough
moulds to make all the
madeleines in one batch, allow
the first batch to cool, wash,
re-grease and re-line the
moulds, and make a further
batch or two.*

While the purists may argue that a meringue is not a cake, it is undoubtedly one of the most delightfully frivolous treats a home-baker can whip up in a domestic kitchen. They have been made for several centuries, and are particularly associated with French pâtisseries. As such, meringues are often viewed as tricky to make, yet nothing could be further from the truth, as the method is simplicity itself.

meringues

FOR THE MERINGUES

3 egg whites
180g caster sugar (unrefined gives the best meringues, but if you are planning on using food colouring, pure white caster sugar is better)
food colouring paste, if you are tinting your meringues (e.g. pink or green)

TO SERVE

250ml double cream, whipped so that it is billowing
fresh raspberries or strawberries

YOU WILL NEED

1 or 2 baking sheets, lined with baking parchment.
NOTE: do not use greaseproof paper as meringues stick to it. Mark 6cm circles spaced apart on the parchment if you need a guide for shape and size

makes 16 individual meringues (8 total when sandwiched with cream)

1/ Preheat the oven to 120°C (gas mark ½).

2/ Put the egg whites into a large, very clean mixing bowl. Stir gently a few times with a fork. Now whisk with an electric mixer until soft peaks form when the whisk is lifted out of the bowl. Do not worry too much about the difference between soft and stiff – as long as your eggs are peaking nicely. Do not over-whisk. If in doubt, stop.

3/ Tip in half the sugar and continue whisking at full speed. After a short while, the mixture will become glossy and shiny. At this point, add the rest of the sugar and whisk well again until all the sugar has been incorporated and the mixture is thick, satiny and glossy.

4/ If colouring, use a toothpick to add the food colouring paste now in very small amounts and whisk again until fully mixed in.

5/ With a dessertspoon, spoon the mix onto the baking sheet, making simple mounds, about 6–10cm wide and 2–4cm high. Swirl or flatten with the back of the spoon if you want them to be meringue nests. Alternatively, for a less vintage, more professional look, use a piping bag with a plain nozzle. (Filling a piping bag can be tricky if you are on your own and have no one to hold the bag while you fill it, in which case stand the nozzle and bag in a jug.)

6/ Bake the meringues in the preheated oven for 1¼ hours or until the meringues have darkened slightly in colour. They should peel off the baking parchment easily and feel light when lifted up.

7/ Whip the cream and use to top individual meringues or to sandwich pairs together. Serve with fresh raspberries and/or strawberries.

variations

• Meringues are already sweet, but using cream sweetened with icing sugar makes them extra delicious. Sift a couple of teaspoons of icing sugar over the cream and whip normally.
• Sweetened cream is particularly good when you add a few raspberries or sliced strawberries into the cream sandwich.

• Alternatively, make individual mini pavlovas and top with cream or sweetened cream and fresh fruit (strawberries, raspberries, nectarines and redcurrants all go well with meringue).

• Coffee meringues are very vintage and have a lovely pale-beige colour. Dissolve 1 teaspoon of coffee powder or granules in 1–2 teaspoons of hot water, and add to the eggs and sugar when whisking.

• Hazelnut meringues have an extra nutty chewiness. Gently fold 25–30g of ground toasted hazelnuts into the whisked egg and sugar mixture just before spooning it out onto the baking sheet.

No one quite knows how éclairs got their name. The word means 'lightning' in French so it may refer to the long shape and the streak of white cream, or the lightning speed with which they are eaten. What is known, though, is that they originated in France in the 19th century, with some food historians speculating that they might be the creation of the legendary chef Antonin Carême. They have been popular ever since, and a plate of fresh éclairs will always disappear in a flash.

éclairs

FOR THE ECLAIRS
150g plain flour
a pinch of salt
120g butter
250ml water
4 eggs, lightly beaten

TO FINISH
300ml double or whipping cream
1–2 tablespoons icing sugar
150g dark chocolate, broken into
  small pieces

YOU WILL NEED
1 or 2 baking sheets, lined with
  baking parchment (or use an éclair
  baking tray, brushed lightly with
  melted butter)
a piping bag with a large plain nozzle
  (optional)

makes 16–20 éclairs

1/ Preheat the oven to 220°C (gas mark 7).
2/ Sift the flour and salt into a bowl. Put the butter and water into a large, heavy-based saucepan. Place over a medium heat until the butter has melted and the mixture begins to bubble. Remove the pan from the heat and immediately add all the flour and salt. Beat vigorously with a wooden spoon or electric whisk until there are no lumps, and the mixture comes away from the sides of the pan.
3/ Gradually add the eggs one by one, beating well after each addition. The mixture should be smooth and glossy, with a thickness similar to wallpaper paste.
4/ Once the mixture is cool enough to handle, either transfer to a piping bag and pipe out lengths of pastry onto the baking sheet, or use a dessertspoon and your fingers to achieve the same effect, creating strips or circles as desired. Make sure you leave plenty of space between the éclairs to allow them to expand during baking. Make in batches if necessary.
5/ Bake in the preheated oven for 15–20 minutes or until puffed up and golden brown. Reduce the temperature to 180°C (gas mark 4) and bake for a further 10–15 minutes. Baking times will vary according to the size of your éclairs, so check during baking.
6/ Remove from the oven and, with a sharp knife, make a small slit in the side or near the base of each éclair to release the steam, and then return to the oven and bake for 3–4 minutes. Remove from the oven, transfer to a wire rack and leave the éclairs to cool completely.
7/ Fill the éclairs just before serving to prevent them going soggy. Put the cream and 1–2 tablespoons of sifted icing sugar (according to taste) into a large mixing bowl. Whip until soft and billowing, but do not over-whip as this makes the cream too stiff. Split each éclair horizontally with a sharp knife and, using a knife or spoon, fill with the sweetened cream.
8/ Melt the chocolate in a bowl over a saucepan of hot water, stirring occasionally and taking care not to get any water in the chocolate. Once melted, spread or drizzle over the éclairs and leave to set.
STORAGE: Eclairs are at their best when fresh and on the day of making.

Butterfly cakes are one of the great little cakes of childhood. They are small enough to be held in the palm of a young hand, yet sufficiently substantial to constitute a proper treat. With their whimsical connotations of butterfly lightness and prettiness, they have an in-built appeal for every new generation of children who will also love making them. They are simply fairy cakes whose tops have been sliced off, cut in two and reapplied as 'wings' on top of a good filling of vanilla or chocolate buttercream. If you add some butterfly 'markings' in the form of favourite little sweets or sprinkles, they are perfect for parties and special occasions.

chocolate butterfly cakes

FOR THE CAKES
105g self-raising flour
30g good-quality cocoa powder
½ teaspoon baking powder
135g soft butter
135g caster sugar
2 eggs

FOR THE ICING
175g icing sugar
30g cocoa powder
65g soft butter
2–3 tablespoons milk, to mix

TO FINISH
sweets or sprinkles, to decorate
   (optional)

YOU WILL NEED
a 12-hole cake or muffin tin and
10–12 paper cases

*makes 12 average or
10 large butterfly cakes*

1/ Preheat the oven to 180°C (gas mark 4). Put 10–12 paper cases in a bun or muffin tin. Measure the flour, cocoa, and baking powder into a small bowl.
2/ Put the butter and sugar in a large mixing bowl. With a wooden spoon or an electric whisk, cream them together until they are pale and fluffy. Add the eggs, one by one, beating well after each addition.
3/ Sift in the dry ingredients and fold in gently with a large spoon until well mixed. Spoon the mix into the paper cases about two-thirds full, taking care to put the same amount in each so the cakes cook evenly.
4/ Bake in the preheated oven for 20 minutes or until risen and springy to the touch and a metal skewer or sharp knife inserted into the centre of the cakes comes out clean. Transfer to a wire rack and leave to cool for 5 minutes before taking the cakes out of the tin.
5/ When the cakes are cold, make the buttercream icing. Sift the icing sugar and cocoa powder into a bowl and add the butter and a little milk (start with a tablespoon). With a handheld electric whisk, wooden spoon or round-ended knife, beat all the ingredients together until thoroughly combined, adding enough milk to make the icing smooth and spreadable.
6/ With a small, sharp knife, slice the tops off the cakes at a slight downward angle, making a little hollow as you do so (rather than cutting straight as you would a boiled egg). Cut each top in half to make 2 'wings'.
7/ Spread each cake with buttercream and replace the wings, right side up, to look like butterflies. Decorate as desired.
STORAGE: Butterfly cakes are delicious when fresh, but can be stored in an airtight tin in a cool place for 1–2 days.

Tipsy cake is a traditional English dessert dating from the 18th century when it was popular at ball suppers. It's an old-fashioned name for what is, essentially, a loose trifle that uses up cake sponge (any of the plain sponges in this book would work). For a truly tipsy effect, add a generous pouring of alcohol such as brandy, sweet sherry or Madeira, or Marsala.

tipsy cake

FOR THE TRIFLES

1 x Victoria sponge cake layer
   (made with 125g each butter, sugar
   and flour, and 2 eggs) – see page 54
   for recipe

medium-dry sherry, Madeira or
   Marsala, for soaking the sponge

fresh fruit or tinned fruit of your
   choice

custard (optional) – use ready-made
   OR make with custard powder OR
   make crème patissiere (see Boston
   Cream Pie, page 165)

whipped cream

decorations, such as silver balls,
   sprinkles, jellied sweets, chocolate
   drops and grated chocolate

YOU WILL NEED

6 trifle dishes or bowls

serves 6

1/ Cut the sponge cake into fingers, or use a biscuit cutter to make shapes, such as stars, flowers or hearts. Arrange them in the base of the trifle bowls.

2/ Pour a generous glug of alcohol over each set of sponges and leave to soak for at least 30 minutes.

3/ Arrange the fresh or tinned fruit on top of the sponges, and pour over a layer of custard (if using). The tipsy cakes can now be kept in the fridge until needed (they will keep a day or so).

4/ When you are ready to serve, whip the cream until it is soft and billowing and spoon over the fruit (and custard, if using). Top with your chosen decorations. If using sprinkles, remember that their colours begin to run once they are damp, so don't add them until just before serving.

STORAGE: Eat tipsy cake immediately.

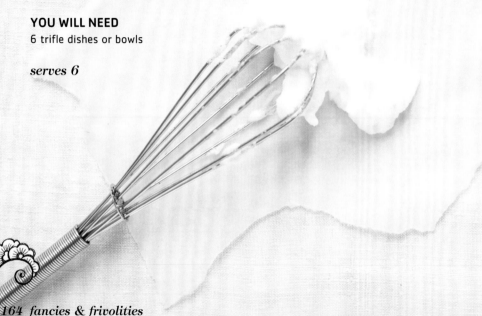

Boston cream pie is not a pie at all: it's a soft sponge cake filled with a layer of vanilla pastry cream or custard and covered with a bittersweet chocolate ganache filling. The 'pie' in the name comes from the fact that in the mid-19th century American home-bakers often used pie tins when baking cakes. With its generous proportions and irresistible combination of textures and tastes, it has become a well-loved fixture on the baking landscape.

boston cream pie

FOR THE CAKES
225g plain flour
2 level teaspoons baking powder
175g soft butter, plus extra
   for greasing
175g caster sugar
1 teaspoon vanilla exract
2 eggs
150ml milk

FOR THE FILLING
150ml double or single cream
150ml milk
1 teaspoon vanilla extract
50g caster sugar
3 egg yolks
2 slightly heaped tablespoons cornflour
a pinch of salt
15g butter

FOR THE TOPPING
150ml double cream
1 teaspoon vanilla extract
10g soft butter
150g good-quality dark chocolate
   (70% cocoa solids), broken
   into small pieces

YOU WILL NEED
two 23cm round sandwich tins, lightly greased with butter and lined with baking parchment

makes 1 large cake
(serves 8–10)

1/ Preheat the oven to 180°C (gas mark 4). To make the sponge: sift the flour and baking powder into a small bowl and set aside. Put the butter and sugar in a large mixing bowl. With a wooden spoon or electric mixer, cream until pale and fluffy. Add the vanilla plus the eggs, one by one, beating well after each addition.
2/ Add the flour mix and the milk in batches, folding in with a large spoon after each addition until you have a well-combined, light mixture. Divide the mix equally between the 2 tins and gently level the surface.
3/ Bake for 25–30 minutes until a metal skewer inserted into the centre of the cake comes out clean. Transfer to a wire rack and leave to cool for 10–15 minutes before turning out. Leave to cool completely before filling and covering.
4/ Make the custard filling. Measure out the cream and milk in a jug and add the vanilla extract. Put the sugar, egg yolks, cornflour and salt in a small bowl. Add 2 tablespoons of the cream mixture and whisk lightly to a smooth consistency. In a small saucepan, gently warm the rest of the cream mixture until bubbles appear round the edges, but do not boil. Pour onto the ingredients in the bowl and whisk well until smooth and lump-free.
5/ Return to the pan and heat gently, stirring to prevent lumps, until the mix thickens to a spreadable consistency. Take off the heat and beat in the butter. Transfer to a small bowl, cover the surface with clingfilm and leave to cool at room temperature. When cool, use to sandwich the two sponge layers.
6/ To make the topping, put all the ingredients in a pan and gently heat until the chocolate has almost melted, stirring occasionally. Take off the heat, leave the chocolate to melt fully and then whisk until thick and smooth. Leave to cool for a few minutes, then spoon over the top of the cake and very gently spread with the back of the spoon so that it covers the surface.
STORAGE: This cake is at its best when freshly made, but will keep for 1–2 days if stored in a cool place (but not the fridge).

These little discs of soft sponge filled with whipped cream and perhaps a smidgen of jam or lemon curd have been popular at tea-time with generations of children and adults in Australia and New Zealand. They are also known as 'powder puffs' on account of their shape and softness, and they are sometimes coloured pastel pink to enhance the comparison. This has the effect of making them even prettier, especially if you put them out on matching china. It's important to let them soften before serving, as this is an integral part of their charm.

sponge kisses

FOR THE CAKES
90g plain flour
15g cornflour
1 teaspoon baking powder
a pinch of salt
2 eggs
120g caster sugar

FOR THE FILLING
about 200ml double cream
lemon curd (see page 141) or jam
icing sugar, to decorate

YOU WILL NEED
2 or 3 baking sheets, lined with
baking parchment

*makes 30 cakes
(15 kisses when
sandwiched
together)*

1/ Preheat the oven to 200°C (gas mark 6).
2/ Sift the dry ingredients, except the sugar, together twice onto a plate and then into a small bowl.
3/ In a large mixing bowl, whisk the eggs with an electric mixer or whisk for 4–5 minutes until pale, thick and moussey. Add the caster sugar in 2 or 3 batches, beating well for 1–2 minutes after each addition. Sift in the dry ingredients. With a large metal spoon or flexible spatula, fold in very gently and carefully until combined.
4/ Make circles of batter by dropping a dessertspoonful at a time onto the lined sheets, keeping the circles well apart. Try to ensure all circles are more or less the same size. Bake in the preheated oven in batches for 6–8 minutes until well risen and pale gold in colour. Transfer to a wire rack and leave to cool for a minute, then lift off the paper with a spatula and leave to cool completely on the rack.
5/ At this point, the cakes can be stored in an airtight tin for 2–3 days. If you are planning to serve them on the day of making, store them for a couple of hours in a tin before filling. This allows them to soften, which is what you want.

6/ To finish the kisses, whip the cream until softly billowing (do not over-whip). Match up the kisses to make pairs. Spread a little lemon curd or jam on one side, cover one side of the other half with whipped cream, and sandwich the two together. Dust with icing sugar when all the kisses have been filled. Make sure you leave 30 minutes between filling the kisses and serving them, as they need time to soften again (this is part of their traditional appeal).
STORAGE: Sponge kisses are best eaten on the day of filling while the cream is still fresh.

Throughout history, cakes have been associated with celebrations and red letter days. Whether it's a birthday or anniversary, a street party, jubilee, or special date in the calendar, there is a cake to match the occasion. Some, like festive cakes, are made to recipes that have been unchanged for decades or centuries, and others, such as birthday cakes, are constantly evolving in appearance, but still serve the same purpose: to bring people together, to share, to celebrate. It's always worth buying the best ingredients you can afford, and to allow plenty of time for preparing the cakes, so that you enjoy the process and have something delicious to show for your time and effort. When it comes to looks, forget minimal, pale and stylish, and think vintage with generous proportions and plenty of lavish decorations. Brightly coloured icing, piped flowers and messages, glacé fruits, hundreds and thousands and silver balls will all bring a sense of glamour and fun to any occasion; they will light up faces, and tell someone they are very special.

celebration
cakes

Simnel cake was not always associated as it now is with Easter. It used to be eaten on the fourth Sunday of Lent, which was known as Simnel or Mothering Sunday. Simnel cake has now moved to a later point in the calendar, but still retains a deep significance, with its 11 balls of marzipan to represent the 12 disciples, minus Judas. It's a celebration of fruit and marzipan; a true family cake. If you omit the marzipan balls, it is a delicious light fruit cake for any time of year.

simnel cake

FOR THE CAKE

500g marzipan
icing sugar, for dusting
400g mixed dried fruit (raisins, sultanas, currants)
50g dried mixed peel
50g glacé cherries, rinsed, drained and halved
finely grated zest of 1 lemon and 1 orange (unwaxed or well washed)
175g plain flour
1 level teaspoon baking powder
½–1 teaspoon spice mix (mixed spice, or a mix of spices, such as ground allspice, grated nutmeg and ground cinnamon
175g soft butter
175g soft light brown sugar
3 eggs
1–2 tablespoons milk
2 tablespoons apricot jam

YOU WILL NEED

a 20cm round cake tin, greased with butter and lined with baking parchment

makes 1 medium–large cake (serves 8–10)

1/ Preheat the oven to 150°C (gas mark 2).
2/ Take 200g of the marzipan and roll out on a work surface dusted with sifted icing sugar into a 20cm disc. To do this, lightly press a 20cm cake tin on the marzipan as your size guide and cut out the circle just inside the line so the disc fits easily on the cake mix when it is in the pan. Keep any leftovers; press and return to the block. Wrap in clingfilm until needed.
3/ Measure out the dried fruit and place with the zest in a bowl. Sift the flour, baking powder and spice(s) into a second bowl. Put the butter and sugar in a large mixing bowl. With a wooden spoon or an electric whisk, cream them together until they are pale and fluffy. Add the eggs one by one, beating well after each addition.
4/ Add the flour mix and the fruit mix, and fold in with a large metal spoon or flexible spatula, adding a little milk to give a smooth consistency. Spoon half the mix into the tin and level the surface with the back of the spoon or spatula. Place the disc of marzipan on top, then spoon in the rest of the cake mix, gently spreading it evenly over the marzipan.
5/ Bake in the preheated oven for 2–2½ hours, until golden brown and well risen. It is not easy to test for doneness because the marzipan sticks to the skewer or knife, so you will have to take an educated guess when inspecting the skewer or knife. Transfer to a wire rack and leave to cool before turning out of the tin. Make sure the cake is completely cool before you move on to the decorating part.
6/ When you are ready to finish the cake, gently warm 2 tablespoons apricot jam in a saucepan until melted. Brush over the surface of the cake. Now weigh out 110g of the marzipan and roll out 11 balls (10g each) then set aside.
7/ On a work surface dusted with icing sugar, roll the remaining marzipan out into a disc to fit on the top of the cake (use the base of the cake tin as a template, and cut round it with a sharp knife). Place the disc on the cake, pinching the edges to make a pattern if desired. Arrange the 11 balls evenly around the cake, using a tiny amount of apricot jam to help them stick and stay in place. Place under a hot grill for 2–3 minutes to brown, taking care not to let the marzipan burn.
STORAGE: Simnel cake will keep for up to a week if wrapped in foil and stored in an airtight tin in a cool place.

iced christmas cake

jewelled christmas cake

Christmas cake is so enshrined in the vintage kitchen calendar that it even has its own special baking day: 'Stir-Up Sunday' which is the last Sunday before Advent. However, your cake will not suffer if you miss this date, and in fact Christmas cake can be made at any time in the run-up to Christmas – there may not be time to age and 'feed' it with alcohol, but it will still taste good. In the past, Christmas cake was often dry, treacly and bitter, but these days paler, more moist versions are more popular, so this is what this recipe offers. You can use any combination of fruits to make the cake, as long as you keep to specified quantities.

jewelled christmas cake

FOR THE CAKE
DAY ONE
1kg of mixed dried fruit (such as
    raisins, currants, sultanas, candied
    lemon and orange peel, glacé
    cherries) – this could be made up
    from 350g raisins, 350g sultanas,
    200g glacé cherries, 50g each lemon
    and orange candied peel
finely grated zest of 1 lemon
finely grated zest and juice of 1 orange
4–6 tablespoons brandy (or your
    preferred spirit), plus extra for
    'feeding'

DAY TWO
100g slivered almonds, chopped, or
    chopped almonds
275g plain flour
½ teaspoon baking powder
¼–½ teaspoon mixed spice
¼–½ teaspoon grated nutmeg
¼ teaspoon salt
250g soft butter, plus extra
    for greasing
250g light or dark muscovado or soft
    brown sugar or 125g of each
4 eggs
1 tablespoon treacle

day one

1/ If possible, it is best to start the day before you plan to bake the cake in order to allow the fruit to soak overnight. If this is not feasible, try to allow the fruit to soak for at least a couple of hours on the day of making.
2/ In a large bowl, put the dried fruit, fresh lemon and orange zest and the soaking juice and alcohol (if using). Mix well to coat all the fruit with liquid. Cover with clingfilm and leave in a cool place overnight. If you can remember, turn the fruit over occasionally to distribute the soaking liquids.

day two

3/ Preheat the oven to 150°C (gas mark 2).
4/ Add the chopped almonds to the soaked fruit and mix in.
5/ In a bowl, measure out the flour, baking powder, spices and salt.
6/ Put the butter and sugar in a large mixing bowl. With a wooden spoon or an electric whisk, cream them together until they are pale and fluffy.
7/ Add the eggs one by one, beating well after each addition. Scrape down the sides of the bowl with a flexible spatula to ensure the ingredients are evenly combined. Add the treacle and stir in lightly – it will be fully mixed in when the other ingredients are added.
8/ Now add the dry ingredients, stir a couple of times and tip in the fruit and any syrupy liquid in the bowl. With a large metal spoon, fold and mix gently but firmly until all the ingredients are combined, making a wish as you do so. Anyone else around at the time should also have a stir and make a wish.
9/ Spoon the mixture into the prepared cake tin, pressing down gently with the back of the spoon to ensure there are no air bubbles, and to smooth and flatten the surface. Bake in the preheated oven for about 2½–3 hours until firm and springy and a metal skewer inserted into the centre comes out clean.

TO COVER

3–4 tablespoons apricot jam or orange marmalade

a selection of fruits and nuts, such as glacé cherries, strips or pieces of candied lemon and orange peel, whole almonds, and pecan and walnut halves

TO DECORATE

length of ribbon (optional)

YOU WILL NEED

a 20cm loose-bottomed cake tin (approx 9cm deep), greased and lined with baking parchment. Wrap a double or triple layer of newspaper or brown paper round the outside of the cake tin and tie tightly with string to prevent the cake burning while cooking. Make sure the paper stands 1–2cm taller than the cake tin.

makes 1 large cake

FOR THE ICED CHRISTMAS CAKE

1 cooked Christmas cake (see pages 174–175)

2–3 tablespoons apricot jam

icing sugar, for dusing

800g marzipan or almond paste

ribbons, tasteful/tasteless ornaments, silver balls, to decorate

FOR THE ICING

2 egg whites

600g icing sugar

2 teaspoons lemon juice

10/ Transfer to a wire rack. Remove the outer wrapping from the tin and leave to cool. When cold, turn the cake out of the tin and remove the baking parchment. Wrap the cake in greaseproof paper. Store in an airtight cake tin or if you don't have a tin, wrap again in aluminium foil.

11/ It is traditional practice to 'feed' the cake with your chosen alcohol once a week or so until Christmas (less frequently if you have made the cake a long time in advance). To do this, use a metal skewer (people used to use darning or butchers' needles) to make holes over the surface of the cake down to the base. Sprinkle a tablespoon or so of alcohol over the cake, rewrap tightly and store.

covering and glazing the cake

12/ You might want to begin by having a practice session of laying out your fruit and nuts in stripes or concentric circles or a star pattern. When you are happy with your layout, get the glaze ready. Gently warm the jam or marmalade in a small pan over a low heat. Sieve and brush the surface of the cake with the jam.

13/ Arrange the fruit and nuts and then carefully brush with the jam or marmalade glaze, making sure all surfaces are covered and shiny. Finish with ribbon if desired.

STORAGE: A rich fruit cake like this keeps well for several weeks if wrapped in foil and stored in an airtight tin in a cool place.

variation: iced christmas cake

1/ Prepare and cook the Christmas cake as for the previous recipe. Once the cake is ready, it can be covered with marzipan and iced on the same day, whenever you are ready to do so in the run-up to Christmas.

2/ Warm 2–3 tablespoons apricot jam in a saucepan over a low heat until it begins to melt. Remove from the heat, stir until thoroughly melted and, if necessary, sieve to remove the fruit and pulp. Brush the top and sides of the cake with the jam.

3/ On a surface lightly dusted with icing sugar, roll out the marzipan or almond paste until you have enough surface area to cover the top and the sides of the cake. Using the cake-tin base as a guide, with a sharp knife cut out a circle of marzipan and place on top of the cake. Now cut out strips of marzipan to fit round the cake, gently pressing into place and joining at the seams.

4/ Make the icing. Put the egg whites in a large mixing bowl. Sift in half the icing sugar and start mixing well with a wooden spoon. When the icing is coming together, sift in the rest of the icing sugar and mix hard again. Add 2 teaspoons of lemon juice and beat again until snowy white and glossy. Leave to rest for a few minutes.

5/ The best way to ice your cake is with a large palette knife dipped in hot water. Place the cake on a covered cake board or stand. Spread the icing as evenly as you can over the top and sides, dipping the knife in the hot water every so often to make the operation smoother and easier. It's difficult to get a very smooth surface with this icing (ready-to-roll icing is better if that is what you want), so make a snowdrift look by swirling and lifting the knife. Decorate as desired.

STORAGE: Store the finished cake in an airtight tin in a cool place.

Also known as a Yule or Christmas log but most closely associated with France and other French-speaking countries, this is the edible version of the real Yule log that was once part of the winter solstice celebrations. It's a light, chocolate sponge filled with buttercream, rolled into a log shape, and iced and decorated to look like a log. It's very easy to make, and even those with absolutely no cake decorating experience will be able to create a very convincing log.

bûche de noël

FOR THE CAKE
butter, for greasing
6 eggs
150g caster sugar
50g cocoa powder
1 teaspoon vanilla extract

FOR THE ICING
150g dark chocolate, broken into
    small pieces
350–400g icing sugar, plus extra
    for dusting
175g soft butter

YOU WILL NEED
a 31 x 21cm Swiss roll tin, greased
with butter and lined with baking
parchment so that the parchment
stands about 5cm taller than the tin

*makes 1 large log
(serves 10–12)*

1/ Preheat the oven to 180°C (gas mark 4).
2/ Separate the eggs, putting the whites in one large mixing bowl, and the yolks in a second large mixing bowl. With a handheld or electric mixer, whisk the egg whites until softly peaking. Add the sugar to the egg yolks, and whisk for 3–4 minutes until pale, light and moussey. Sift in the cocoa powder, add the vanilla extract and fold in gently with a large metal spoon or flexible spatula.
3/ Now add a spoonful of egg whites at a time, carefully folding in until all the ingredients are combined and there are no streaks of white. Handle the mix as gently as possible in order to avoid knocking out the air.
4/ Pour into the prepared tin and bake in the preheated oven for 20 minutes, by which time the sponge will be very well risen, pulling away from the edges of the tin and firm to the touch. Transfer to a wire rack and leave to cool for a few minutes.
5/ While the cake is cooling, cut out a piece of baking parchment which is larger than the cake and dust with icing sugar. Turn the cake out onto the sheet of parchment, gently pulling at the lining to help it come out of the tin. Peel off the parchment, cover with a tea towel and leave to cool before trimming the edges.
6/ When you are ready, make the buttercream icing. Put the chocolate pieces into a small bowl set over a pan of just-boiled water. Leave to melt, stirring occasionally. Sift 350g icing sugar into a mixing bowl and add the butter and melted chocolate. Mix well, adding more icing sugar to achieve a spreadable consistency.
7/ With a palette knife, spread a layer of buttercream over the surface of the cake. Then, with the wider side of the cake facing you, lift up the parchment and carefully roll up the cake, using the parchment to help pull it into a roll and pressing gently but firmly on the parchment to make it even. Place the cake, seam down, on your chosen serving plate or board.
8/ Now you can be creative with your log. Make sawn-off branches by cutting off one or both ends of the log at an angle and replacing them along the side of the main log. Use the buttercream to 'glue' the branch(es) to the log, before covering the entire log, ends included if desired, with the icing. Make bark markings along the log and wood rings at the ends with a metal skewer or fork. The log can be stored in an airtight tin in a cool place for up to 5 days.
9/ When ready to serve, dust generously with icing sugar and decorate if desired, according to taste. Serve with pouring or lightly whipped cream if you wish.
STORAGE: The log is best eaten within a week of making, but should be stored in a cool place at all times.

The importance of a cake in any kind of traditional celebration cannot be underestimated, and even in more straitened times, bakers have always made economies and done their best to ensure that there is something impressive and breathtaking to cut and share. It need not be fancy or difficult to make; more important are the scale and decorations. This celebration cake can be adapted to suit any special occasion, based as it is on a simple sponge recipe which can be multiplied as necessary. Then all you need to do is decide on your theme and colour scheme, and have fun making it.

celebration cake

FOR THE CAKES (makes 3 layers)
375g soft butter, plus extra
    for greasing
375g caster sugar
6 eggs, lightly beaten
½ teaspoon good-quality vanilla
    extract
375g self-raising flour
1–2 tablespoons whole milk

FOR THE ICING
200g soft butter
500–600g icing sugar
2–3 tablespoons milk, to mix
food colouring paste (optional)
a few drops of vanilla extract (optional)

TO DECORATE
a mix of 'vintage' sweets or cake decorations to suit the occasion

YOU WILL NEED
three 20cm round loose-bottomed sandwich tins, greased with butter and bases lined with baking parchment

makes 1 very large cake
(serves 12–16)

1/ Preheat the oven to 180°C (gas mark 4).
2/ Place the butter and sugar in a large mixing bowl. Cream them together until very pale and fluffy. Allow at least 2 minutes with an electric whisk for this, more if you are mixing by hand. Every so often, scrape down the sides with a flexible spatula to ensure everything is evenly mixed.
3/ Gradually add the lightly beaten eggs and vanilla extract, mixing well after each addition, until all the eggs have been added. Mix until the mixture is pale and fluffy.
4/ Sift the flour into the bowl. Using a large metal spoon, very gently fold in the flour, gradually adding the milk to give a very light, fluffy consistency.
5/ Divide the mixture between the 3 prepared sponge tins. (Use electronic scales for accuracy.) Smooth the surfaces with the back of the spoon. Bake the cakes, in batches if necessary, in the preheated oven for 20–25 minutes. The cakes are ready when they are firm to the touch, are pulling away from the sides and a metal skewer or sharp knife inserted into the centre of the cakes comes out clean.
6/ Transfer to a wire rack and leave to cool for a few minutes before turning out. Leave to cool before filling, covering and decorating. If necessary, level the surfaces of the sponge cakes with a sharp knife.
7/ To make the buttercream icing, put the butter into a large mixing bowl and sift in 500g icing sugar. Add 2 tablespoons milk and a small amount of food colouring paste or vanilla (if using) and beat well with a wooden spoon or electric mixer until you have a soft, smooth, spreadable consistency. Add a little more milk or icing sugar if necessary to obtain the taste and consistency you like.
8/ Place the bottom layer of sponge upside down on a cake stand or plate and with a palette knife cover with a layer of buttercream. Place the next layer of sponge on top also upside down and cover with buttercream. Repeat with the third layer, the right way up. Cover with buttercream and decorate as you please.
STORAGE: This cake can be baked and decorated a day in advance and should be stored in a cool place until needed. It will keep well for 1–2 days after baking.

In Britain, little sponge cakes with pretty icing and decorations have long been known affectionately as 'fairy cakes'. It's not a technical term, but rather one befitting children's birthday parties, balloons and streamers, silver balls and hundreds and thousands, and pastel icing that can be licked off before the sponge is tackled (or, depending on how old you are, discarded). They are delightfully easy to make, and a wonderful way of introducing children to baking. These days we have many more colours, decorations and sprinkles at our disposal to transform simple baking into a colourful, creative activity.

fairy cakes

FOR THE CAKES
125g soft butter
125g caster sugar
2 eggs
125g self-raising flour
a few drops of vanilla extract (optional)
1-2 tablespoons milk, to mix

YOU WILL NEED
a 12-hole bun tin, lined with 12 paper
  cases

makes 12 fairy cakes

1/ Preheat the oven to 180°C (gas mark 4).
2/ Put the butter and sugar in a large mixing bowl. With a wooden spoon or an electric whisk, cream them together until they are pale and fluffy. This will take a couple of minutes. Scrape down the sides of the bowl with a flexible spatula to bring the mixture together several times during beating.
3/ Add the eggs one by one, continuing to beat well after each addition. If the mixture starts to curdle or separate you can add a tablespoon of flour and mix again, although this is not strictly necessary.
4/ When the eggs have been beaten in, add the flour and with a metal spoon or flexible spatula, gently fold into the mix until well combined. Add a tablespoon of milk, or more if needed, and mix gently to give a soft consistency.
5/ Use a dessertspoon to spoon the mix into the paper cases, dividing it equally and filling them two-thirds full. Bake in the preheated oven for 15–20 minutes until well risen and golden brown on top.
6/ Transfer to a wire rack and leave to cool for a few minutes before turning the cakes out of the tin. Leave to cool completely before icing. Ice and decorate with your chosen icing and toppings (see page 183).
STORAGE: Fairy cakes are best eaten on the day of making, but will keep for a day or two in an airtight tin in a cool place.

iced fairy cakes with sprinkles

iced fairy cakes

iced fairy cakes with silver balls

decorating variations: white icing with a cherry on top

1/ Sift the icing sugar into a bowl and gradually add the liquid sparingly while mixing. Take care not to add too much liquid too soon or you will have to add large amounts of icing sugar to compensate and end up with vast quantities of icing. With a knife or flexible spatula, mix well adding more liquid or icing sugar if necessary to achieve a thick, shiny, lump-free, spreadable icing.

2/ If you prefer, make the tops of the cakes flat by slicing off the rounded top before icing (taking care that the sponge crumbs do not get mixed up in the icing).

3/ Using a round-ended or small palette knife, spread the icing on the cakes and decorate each fairy cake with half a bright-red glacé cherry.

cherry-topped iced fairy cakes

cook's tip

Lemon or orange juice will give a very pale tinge of colour to icing, which won't show if you plan to colour the icing with food colouring.

coloured icing with sprinkles & sweets

1/ Sift the icing sugar into a bowl and gradually add the liquid (water, lemon juice or orange juice) to mix. Take care not to add too much liquid too soon. Using a knife or spatula, mix well, adding tiny amounts of food colouring paste to get the shade and depth of colour you require. Add more liquid or icing sugar if necessary to achieve a thick, smooth, shiny, spreadable icing.

2/ Using a round-ended or small palette knife, spread the icing on the cakes and decorate each one with your choice of sprinkles and/or sweets.

Stollen is a traditional fruity, spicy German bread baked at Christmas, although it's too good to be restricted to just one time of the year. It's a heavyweight bread packed with fruits, peel, spice and marzipan. It looks very festive dredged in snowy icing sugar, but as it is light in sugar, it is not over-rich. It takes some time to make, but the end result is spectacular, and suitably good for sharing or giving.

stollen

FOR THE CAKE

225g mixed dried fruit (such as 125g sultanas, 75g raisins and 25g mixed candied peel)

30g almonds, chopped (or use flaked almonds, chopped)

grated zest of 1 orange

2 tablespoons rum

75g caster sugar

375g strong plain flour, plus extra for dusting

1 x 7g sachet fast-action dried yeast

1 teaspoon salt

spice (optional and to taste), such as a good grating of nutmeg plus a pinch of ground cardamom OR ½ teaspoon ground cinnamon, OR ½ teaspoon mixed spice

150g lukewarm milk

75g melted butter

1 egg

250g marzipan

TO FINISH

65g melted butter

icing sugar, for dusting

YOU WILL NEED

1 baking sheet, lined with baking parchment

makes 1 large stollen (serves 10–12)

1/ In a bowl, mix the dried fruit, chopped almonds, orange zest and rum. Leave to stand while making the dough.

2/ Put the sugar, flour, dried yeast, salt and spice into a large mixing bowl. Add the milk, butter and egg, and the dried fruit and almond mix. Combine well with your hand or a flexible spatula to form a sticky dough, adding a little more milk if the mix is too dry (although this is very unlikely).

3/ Turn the dough out onto a well-floured work surface, and knead gently for 3–5 minutes until smooth and elastic. Form into a ball. Lightly oil the mixing bowl (it doesn't need to be washed before you do this), put the dough in and cover with clingfilm or a damp tea towel. Leave in a warm place to rise for 2–3 hours until it has doubled in size.

4/ Turn the dough out onto a floured work surface and knead a few times to knock out the air. Roll out into a rectangle, about 28cm long and 20cm wide. Place the rectangle of dough on the baking sheet.

5/ Roll the marzipan into a tube or sausage shape, about 26cm long. Press down on it gently to squash into an oval shape. Place the marzipan roll on the dough, slightly to one side of the centre. Fold the wider side of the dough over the marzipan, and press it down on the other side to make a seam. Cover with lightly oiled clingfilm and leave to rise for 1 hour. While the stollen is rising, preheat the oven to 180°C (gas mark 4).

6/ After 1 hour, remove the clingfilm and bake for 30–40 minutes until risen and golden brown. As soon as the Stollen comes out of the oven, brush it with 50g melted butter. Leave to cool.

7/ Once it is completely cool, brush again with the remaining melted butter and dust thickly with icing sugar.

STORAGE: Wrap in foil and store in a cool place. Stollen is delicious fresh, but keeps well for 3–4 days.

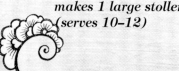

Although there is no authentic Valentine's cake as such, it's a time-honoured occasion that can be celebrated with a heart-shaped cake. Inspired by pretty vintage cards featuring hearts and roses, this cake can be dressed up as little or as much as you like with coloured icing, floral decorations, or even hand-piped declarations of love. The sponge contains buttermilk and keeps well for several days, so the cake can be made in advance. It also works well as a birthday cake.

valentine's cake

FOR THE CAKE
275g plain flour
½ teaspoon baking powder
½ teaspoon bicarbonate of soda
½ teaspoon salt
finely grated zest of 1 lemon (unwaxed or well washed)
125g butter
220g caster sugar
3 eggs
200ml buttermilk
2 teaspoons lemon juice
a small amount of pink or red food colouring paste (optional)
sugar flowers, sprinkles, sweets, silver balls, to decorate

FOR THE ICING
200–250g icing sugar
lemon juice or water, to mix
food colouring paste (optional)

YOU WILL NEED
a springform heart-shaped tin, about 24cm wide and 7cm deep, greased with butter and base lined with baking parchment

makes 1 large heart-shaped cake (serves 18–20)

1/ Preheat the oven to 180°C (gas mark 4).
2/ Sift the flour, baking powder, bicarbonate of soda and salt into a bowl. Add the grated lemon zest and stir to mix.
3/ Put the butter and sugar in a large mixing bowl. With a wooden spoon or an electric whisk, cream them together until they are pale and fluffy. Add the eggs one by one, beating well after each addition.
4/ Add half the flour mix, half the buttermilk, plus the lemon juice and a little food colouring (if using), and fold in gently with a large metal spoon. Add the rest of the flour and buttermilk and continue to fold in until thoroughly and evenly combined, adding more pink or red colouring paste to get the shade you require. Spoon the mixture into the prepared tin and level the surface with the back of the spoon.
5/ Bake in the preheated oven for 50–55 minutes, but check the cake after 30–35 minutes to make sure it is not browning too quickly. If it is, place a double thickness of aluminium foil over the tin. The cake is ready when a metal skewer or sharp knife inserted into the centre comes out clean. Transfer to a wire rack and leave to cool. Remove from the tin, and leave to cool completely before icing.
6/ To make the glacé icing: sift 200g icing sugar into a bowl. Add a small amount of liquid and colouring paste (if using). With a knife or spatula, begin mixing, gradually adding more liquid until you have a smooth, not-too-runny icing that drops slowly off the spoon. Add more icing sugar and food colouring if necessary to obtain the required consistency and shade.
7/ To finish the cake, place it on a plate, stand or board and carefully level the surface of the cake by cutting off any excess, domed sponge with a serrated knife. (This is not essential and only needs to be done if you want a flat top to your cake.)
8/ With a palette knife, carefully spread the icing over the top of the cake, pushing it gently towards the edges and allowing it to run over the side if liked.
9/ As soon as you have finished icing the cake and before the icing or buttercream begins to set, decorate as desired.
STORAGE: Buttermilk cake keeps well for 2 days after making and can be made in advance and decorated just before serving. Wrap in foil and store in an airtight tin in a cool place.

You may not guess from its extravagant appearance, but red velvet cake is deliciously light and extremely moreish. Already a classic in America, especially in the southern states, it's now becoming more widely known as more people realise that its looks, taste, and keeping qualities make it a fabulous birthday or celebration cake. Although these days the deep-red colour is achieved with food colouring, it was originally the product of the reaction of the acidic vinegar and buttermilk with the colouring compounds in the cocoa, all of which made baking the cake a fascinating chemistry lesson. It's important to be brave with the food colouring as the mix is meant to be wickedly red.

red velvet cake

FOR THE CAKE
120g soft butter
300g caster sugar
2 eggs
1 teaspoon vanilla extract
300g plain flour
10g cocoa powder
1 teaspoon salt
220g buttermilk
1–2 teaspoons red food colouring
    paste (or more)
1 tablespoon white wine vinegar
1 heaped teaspoon bicarbonate of soda

FOR THE FROSTING
110g soft butter
400g icing sugar
220g soft cream cheese
a few drops of vanilla extract
pink and/or red sprinkles (optional),
    to decorate

YOU WILL NEED
two 20cm round sandwich tins, greased with butter and lined with baking parchment or greaseproof paper

makes 1 large cake (serves 10)

1/ Preheat the oven to 160°C (gas mark 3).
2/ Put the butter and sugar in a large mixing bowl. With a wooden spoon or an electric whisk, cream them together until they are pale and fluffy.
3/ Add the eggs one by one, and a few drops of vanilla extract, beating well after each addition.
4/ Sift the flour, cocoa powder and salt into the bowl in batches and fold in gently with a large metal spoon, adding the buttermilk gradually in between the batches of flour.
5/ Now add the red colouring until you have a deep-red batter – do not be tempted to stay pale, this needs to be truly red. But be careful not to overdo it as it will darken and brown in the oven. Fold in gently until the mix is all one colour.
6/ Mix together the vinegar and bicarbonate of soda and add to the mixture, folding in and combining the ingredients thoroughly.
7/ Divide the mixture between the 2 tins and bake in the preheated oven for 25–30 minutes (mine were done after 27 minutes) until the cakes are firm, springy and pulling away from the sides of the tin, and a metal skewer or sharp knife inserted into the centre of the cakes comes out clean.
8/ Transfer to a wire rack to cool. Remove from the tins after 5–10 minutes and leave to cool completely before icing.
9/ Now make the frosting. Put the butter in a mixing bowl, and sift over the icing sugar. Cream together with an electric whisk or wooden spoon until smooth. Add the cream cheese and a few drops of vanilla extract and mix thoroughly until pale, smooth and spreadable. Check the taste and adjust if necessary.
10/ Place one of the cake layers upside down on a plate or cake stand so you have a nice, flat surface. Spread with the frosting. Put the other cake layer on top, the right way up. Carefully slice off the dome with a long, sharp knife if you want a flat surface. Use the remaining frosting to cover the top and sides.
STORAGE: Red velvet cake is delicious on the day it is made, but also keeps extremely well for 2–3 days if stored in an airtight tin in a cool place.

index

useful addresses

As vintage cakes originated in times when ingredients were less varied and kitchen equipment was more basic, they generally depend on relatively few ingredients and minimal specialised equipment. In fact, you can buy everything you need for all but a few cakes in this book in most major supermarkets and homeware shops. These days, supermarkets offer extensive ranges of all the staple ingredients (butter, sugar, eggs, flour) as well as the important additional ingredients (spices, chocolate, jam, syrup, treacle, raising agents, flavour extracts). And now they have better-than-ever selections of the lovely finishing touches (decorations, paper cases, icing sugars). As many have also started selling essential cooking and baking equipment, you really don't need to go far to find what you need. Alternatively, John Lewis, Debenhams, House of Fraser and BHS are good-value stockists of equipment.

SPECIAL INGREDIENTS:
There are a few ingredients that were once widely available but are now difficult to find, plus several more modern baking ingredients that are worth seeking out.

WHOLE FOODS and HOLLAND & BARRETT and other health food shops are good for malt extract and fine oatmeal.
www.wholefoodsmarket.com
www.hollandandbarrett.com

KINGDOM or DEVON GOLD label curd cheese is available in larger branches of the major supermarkets. It is also sometimes sold at the deli or cheese counter of supermarkets. Or try a good deli (Polish delicatessens usually sell curd cheese).

BART SPICES sell a good range of spices by mail order.
www.bartspices.com
Alternatively, most supermarkets offer a good range of ground and whole spices, but markets and specialist Asian food shops are great places for cheap quantities of individual spices if you use them frequently.

LAKELAND is always worth looking at for good-quality flavour extracts.
www.lakeland.co.uk

AMAZON is also worth looking at for good-quality vanilla and almond extracts and also food colouring pastes.
www.amazon.co.uk

WILTON and SUGARFLAIR are the widely available brands of food colouring paste, which comes in so many brilliant colours that there is no need for the pale, watery food colouring liquids.
www.wilton.com

CAKE CRAFT SHOP sells Wilton food colouring pastes.
www.cakecraftshop.co.uk

CAKE CRAFT WORLD sells Sugarflair food colouring pastes.
www.cakecraftworld.co.uk

THE SUGAR SHACK has a range of pastes on offer.
www.sugarshack.co.uk

SQUIRE'S KITCHEN sells its own brand of paste in an amazing range of colours.
www.squires-shop.com

CAKES, COOKIES & CRAFTS is a treasure trove of decorations and fripperies.
www.cakescookiesandcraftsshop.co.uk
(All these websites are also good for cake decorating supplies.)

EQUIPMENT:
The following all stock general baking equipment as well as more specialised items:

JOHN LEWIS
www.johnlewis.com

LAKELAND is brilliant for tins and trays, as well as huge rolls of baking parchment, cake-tin liners and basic decorating equipment.
www.lakeland.co.uk

THE SUGAR SHACK
www.sugarshack.co.uk

JANE ASHER
www.janeasher.com

SILVERWOOD
www.alansilverwood.co.uk

MORE DIFFICULT-TO-FIND ITEMS:
De Cuisine and Divertimenti stock Angel Food/tube tins and madeleine trays.
www.decuisine.co.uk
www.divertimenti.co.uk

NISBETS and AMAZON have dariole moulds.
www.nisbets.co.uk
www.amazon.co.uk

KITCHEN CRAFT sells a wide range of silicone moulds.
www.kitchencraft.co.uk

VINTAGE CHINA, CUTLERY, KITCHENWARE AND TEXTILES:
Vintage china and textiles are becoming increasingly sought-after, which means you need to be wary of being overcharged by sellers. It's still possible to find plenty of wonderful bone china, beautiful vintage cutlery and cheerful hand-embroidered tablecloths at bargain prices if you are prepared to do the seeking out yourself. It also has to be said that eBay is an amazing place for vintage finds. However, vintage kitchenware is already expensive, as are some very collectible designs of china, and anything 'mid-century modern' is going up in price, which puts it beyond the budget of most non-specialist collectors.

The best way to build up an assortment of vintage items is to buy the things you like at a price that seems fair and reasonable, rather than looking for specific pieces; that way you are more likely to have pleasant surprises and happy coincidences, and a healthier bank balance. One of the great charms of 'vintage style' is that an element of deliberate mismatching looks good, which means it's worth buying individual items as you find them, rather than waiting to chance upon a full set.

The best places for good-value vintage homeware are charity shops, flea markets, antiques fairs, weekend street markets and local auction houses, and eBay (www.ebay.co.uk) is fantastic for browsing in the comfort of your own home. The BBC's 'Homes and Antiques' magazine has useful listings of many antiques fairs.

acknowledgements

Many thanks to Jacqui Small and Jo Copestick for their vision and flair, to Kerenza Swift who did an amazing job of co-ordinating all the elements of the book and keeping everything on track, and to Abi Waters who brought her careful eye to bear on the recipes and text.

Creating this book has been very much a team effort, and I was incredibly fortunate to work with three very talented people during the photoshoots. I am delighted to have Polly Wreford's beautiful photographs of my cakes in this book, and I must also thank her for seeking out and turning up some great vintage bargains. I'd also like to thank Malcolm Menzies who was Polly's hard-working assistant, and I am enormously grateful to Sarah Rock who not only kept all the shoots on course, but also contributed many lovely visual and styling details, and is responsible for the fabulous design of the book.

Jane Graham Maw and Jennifer Christie at Graham Maw Christie have been as helpful and as generous with advice as ever, and I thank them for all their support.

I also want to acknowledge and thank the people who have been encouraging me to bake since I could first stand on a stool to help my Nana in her kitchen. When I was growing up, my Mum let me have free run of her kitchen and larder, and my siblings – Roger, Matthew and Kate – were always willing consumers. Ever since I met him, my husband Simon has been happy to eat what I bake, so a cake book was welcomed, and he has been wonderfully patient and understanding during the hard work it has entailed – I can't thank him enough. As for our three children, they have been stalwart supporters ever since they could sit on a kitchen work surface and help me bake cakes. Thank you, Tom and Alice.

And Phoebe, of course. Phoebe is my right-hand woman in the kitchen, my recipe-checker, a reliably calm, firm and sensible presence, and a very entertaining one, too. She is a natural, creative baker who has helped and inspired me throughout the writing of this book, and I dedicate it to her with many thanks, and much love.